# PRACTICING BUSINESS

# PRACTICING BUSINESS

## Communication in the Workplace

## James VanOosting

Southern Illinois University at Carbondale

**HOUGHTON MIFFLIN COMPANY    BOSTON**

**DALLAS ● GENEVA, ILLINOIS ● PALO ALTO ● PRINCETON, NEW JERSEY**

Book design: Carol H. Rose

Printed in the U.S.A.

Library of Congress Catalog Card Number: 91-71954

ISBN: 0-395-56496-4

ABCDEFGHIJ-D-9987654321

For My Father

# CONTENTS

Preface    ix

Introduction    1

## PART ONE

### ..................... Business Writing and Reading    11

Experienced Expediter Wanted    *13*

To Whom Are You Speaking?    *20*

Ghostwriting 1: Letter Composition    *24*

Get the Point? Creating a Pencil Ad    *27*

A Chain Letter    *30*

Ghostwriting 2: Speech Composition    *35*

A Close Call    *38*

Politics and Profits: A Contested Policy    *46*

## PART TWO

### ..................... Business Speaking and Listening    51

A Language Scavenger Hunt    *53*

Hospital-ity: A Two-Party Negotiation    *58*

Computer Game Sales Conference    *65*

Debate 1: Educational Philosophy    *69*

"It's My Party": A Case of Mistaken Identity    *73*

Debate 2: Management Cross-Examination    *78*

Up in Smoke: A Three-Party Negotiation    *81*

## PART THREE

...................... **Interviewing and Small Groups    87**

Job Interview 1: "Meet the Management"    *89*

Job Interview 2: One-on-One    *95*

Job Negotiation: High-Risk Interviews    *98*

Exit Interview    *103*

Affirmative Inaction    *109*

The Case of Infectious Research    *113*

Helping Hands: A Community Trust    *117*

A Sweet Deal Turned Sour: A Problem for the Graff Candy
   Company    *121*

In Whose Best Interest?    *126*

## PART FOUR

...................... **Media and Technology    131**

Telephone Solicitation    *133*

Selling Business 1: Radio Spots    *136*

See the World — On Radio    *139*

Selling Business 2: TV Spots    *142*

TV Talk Show    *146*

Video Résumé    *150*

Video Franchising    *154*

Video Trainer    *159*

# PREFACE

*Practicing Business: Communication in the Workplace* presents thirty-two interactive situations for experiencing real-world issues of business communication. These cases challenge students to combine their experience — work in organizations, technical knowledge, critical thinking skills, and common sense — with their creativity to solve the kinds of communication problems that any manager or executive might encounter throughout a career.

Representing a range of business environments from manufacturing to service and a variety of business players from clerical staff to CEOs, these training scenarios help students to achieve business success through thinking critically and acting decisively. In each situation, students confront a communication problem in its business context and then work individually or collaboratively to implement an effective solution. Every scenario proceeds logically from a brief introduction (stating a learning objective), to a workplace scene (detailing a specific situation), to a problem (posing a conflict), to an assignment (suggesting step-by-step activities for addressing that problem), to documentation (presenting business papers and worksheets).

By simulating workplace situations, *Practicing Business* creates a lively, participatory environment for learning and teaching business communication. In addition, the book includes

○ FYI boxes that provide background information essential to completing selected assignments

○ Reproductions of business documents such as memos, letters, press releases, personnel forms, and report graphics that provide primary source material

○ Strategic Planning and Job Appraisal forms that provide checklists and fill-ins for preparing and evaluating assignments

The scenarios in *Practicing Business* draw on composites from real-life experience, although none replicates a factual circumstance. They comprise a laboratory for testing organizational theories on the job and for experimenting with the practices of business communication. Interactive simulations help to make learning explicit, tangible, and memorable.

## ACKNOWLEDGMENTS

Most of the workplace situations in this book have been tested, some repeatedly, in university classrooms and professional settings. They owe much to the comments and recommendations of students, workshop participants, and business clients. For the simulation entitled "A Sweet Deal Turned Sour," I thank Dr. Mary Pelias. For their research assistance, I thank graduate students Tim Hood, Craig Gingrich-Philbrook, and Christine Broda. For their helpful readings of the book in manuscript, I thank

William James Buchholz, *Bentley College*

David P. Dauwalder, *California State University, Los Angeles*

Penny Hirsch, *Northwestern University*

Melinda Knight, *New York University*

Grant T. Savage, *Texas Tech University*

For sharing with me the challenges of organizational life and the satisfactions of a working community, I thank my colleagues in the Department of Speech Communication, Southern Illinois University at Carbondale. And finally, for their creativity and support, I thank the staff at Houghton Mifflin.

JVO

# INTRODUCTION

# M E M O R A N D U M

**TO:** **The Student**

**FROM:** **JVO**

Your ability to communicate in business and professional settings is the single greatest predictor of personal success in a
career. Communication can bond or break relationships. It can
build or destroy morale. It can clarify or cloud mission, purpose,
and strategy. It can yield profits or ensure losses.

Communication is the most important commodity produced
and service rendered within any business or profession. Without
reliable communication skills, you cannot realize your highest
potential. The rewards of personal achievement depend as
much upon your ability to communicate in the workplace as
they do upon technical know-how, financial wizardry, or other
specialized training.

That's what this book is all about — helping you to attain practical, reliable communication skills, based on fundamental principles, and applying directly to business and professional settings.
To get the most out of this study, I hope you'll bring  to it all of
your experience: the content of other courses, the disciplines
of thinking honed throughout your education, the technical
knowledge gained from specialized training and, above *all,* your
practical experience of organizations — employment, civic and
volunteer organizations, religious and cultural communities,
and social agencies. In addition, I challenge you to balance common sense with imagination when probing the complexities of
business and organizational communication.

Communication takes place between people. That simple statement has far-reaching consequences. Think about how communication works within your own family, among your friends, and at the workplace, and you will soon conclude that the communication process is anything but easy to understand. You can study principles of communication, but no rules will ensure success in every situation. Likewise, you can consider organizational theories, but no intellectual code will govern all practice. Communication reflects the diversity, mystery, and idiosyncrasy of individuals.

*Communication is interaction through which two or more individuals share meaning or achieve common understanding.*

Let's look at just the first part of this definition — communication is interaction — and tease out some implications. Communication demands participation, interaction, involvement between two or more individuals. And individuals are just that — separate, different, unique. Every participant in a communication situation has an individual way of looking at things. Each one dresses differently, uses a personalized vocabulary, comes from a particular social and economic background, reflects special education and training, displays unique values, and is motivated by different needs, desires, and fears. Understanding how communication works begins with the assumptions that people are different and that interaction between them demands some back-and-forth, some give-and-take.

The second part of the definition lays out the goal of communication: to achieve shared meaning or common understanding. Interaction aims to reduce distance, to negotiate difference, and to ease involvement. If an older person is to communicate with a younger one, both individuals must find a way to get beyond the differences imposed by their ages. If a man and a woman are to communicate, both individuals must use a vocabulary that allows mutual participation. If racial differences are to be negotiated, individuals must be willing to see things from another's vantage point. If management and labor are to interact, they must create a common ground of mutual interest. If manufacturer and customer are to communicate, they must understand one another's needs and limitations.

Communication is hard work, and necessarily so. To interact with anyone different from yourself, to create common understanding, requires you to yield some of your autonomy. You can never communicate with another person without giving something of yourself to the interaction. In return, you may expect some flexibility from the other person. The dividends of communication accrue to participants in direct proportion to their personal investments in the process.

This definition of *communication* — interacting with the aim of understanding — rules out several other possible uses of the word. It cannot mean simply talking. The mere mouthing of words, without a commitment to achieving shared meaning, is noise, not communication. Nor does our definition permit the idea of one individual controlling another or imposing one's will forcibly on another. That is coercion, not communication. More subtly, communication must be visualized as one person simply transmitting some message to another. Transmission and interaction are two different processes. Transmission is a one-way operation; interaction is reciprocal. Transmission assumes sameness between the sender and the receiver; interaction acknowledges differences.

Communication is a creative collaboration. It does not just happen; it is made. It is never a solo recital; it is always an ensemble performance. Communication rules out the hostile takeover of one individual by another; it encourages a negotiated merger. Communication is radically democratic and participatory. It respects individual rights while forging shared understandings. To participate in any communication process, you must make a mutual commitment to yourself and to others.

## LANGUAGE AND RELATIONSHIPS

Meaning resides in persons and relationships, not in words. Even the simplest term can take on different meanings depending on who says it, to whom, and under what circumstances. "I'm hungry" issuing from the mouth of a four-year-old probably means "I want food." The same words, "I'm hungry," spoken by a college sophomore at midnight during final exam week might mean "I'm bored with studying. Let's get a pizza." From a person struggling to lose weight, "I'm hungry" can be a painful admission of the difficulty of dieting. A starving child near death uses the same words as a joyful mother after giving birth: "I'm hungry." A masked gunman points a revolver at a grocery store clerk and says, "I'm hungry." The giant in a fairy tale licks his chops at the sight of a little child and bellows, "I'm hungry." A witch opening her oven door cackles the same lethal threat: "I'm hungry." A football coach, rallying enthusiasm among his defensive players, asks, "Are you hungry?" In unison, they yell back, "We're hungry." Under still other circumstances, in different relationships, "I'm hungry" might refer to ambition, to appetites other than for food, or to some other personal desire. The same words can be informative, persuasive, comic, satiric, beguiling, or threatening.

No dictionary will tell you all of these meanings for *hunger*. You can figure them out only by reference to a particular relationship within a certain set of circumstances. Meaning resides in people and their relationships, not in words. To illustrate this point, try the following exercise.

Imagine that you have just received a job offer representing career advancement, a $10,000 annual increase over your current salary, and the demand that you move to any of six desirable locations. Given these personal and professional advantages, you decide to accept the offer. Now, consider how you will announce your decision to various people. Try to place yourself in the actual circumstances, and imagine the exact words you will use to tell each of the following persons that you have decided to take the new job and will be moving:

1. How will you tell your current boss?
2. How will you tell your future boss?
3. How will you tell your parents, who live in the town where you now live?
4. How will you tell your best friend at work?
5. How will you tell your best friend from college days?
6. How will you tell your six-year-old child, who is enjoying first grade?

Notice how the roles you play in these different relationships influence your language choices and the relative importance you place on each item of information. In addition, you are likely to employ different tones of voice and even, perhaps, different media (for example, face-to-face interaction, telephone, or letter) as you consider what communication options are most appropriate to each relationship.

Both the potentials and the problems of business communication derive from the same source: the differences between one person's intention and another's perception. *Intention* refers to an individual's conscious aim in communication, some desired result that the communicator has in mind. *Perception* refers to an individual's conscious or unconscious recognition of someone else. What you want to say (your intention) may be quite different from what I hear you saying (my perception). How you want to appear (intention) may not be the way I see you (perception). When one person's perceptions match another's intentions, the result is a solid relationship; communication is easy, and understanding is possible. However, when one person's intention and another's perception do not match up, the relationship is jeopardized, interaction is hard, and mutual understanding is impossible. The difficult work of communication is to reduce the distance between intention and perception, to negotiate the differences. This work requires self-awareness and commitment.

## TRAINING SCENARIOS: A WAY OF LEARNING

Coming to terms with business and organizational communication *in theory* is hard enough. Grasping principles *in practice* is even more difficult. Yet doing both is the bottom line of professional competence. When you interview for an entry-level management position, the company wants to know what you have *done*. A potential employer is interested in the transcript of classes that you have taken, of course, but even more interested in the résumé of your experiences. The thirty-two training scenarios in this book open a door onto real-world situations leading you across the threshold from lecture hall to workplace. The way you will learn here, through simulation and role-playing, is significantly different from reading a textbook and taking an exam; yet the two approaches are related.

This book offers laboratory experiences, allowing hands-on participation in business and professional communication. Training scenarios, like any other instance of human creativity, require time, get messy, and cause frustration. Their short-term worth can be measured by how you apply theoretical principles to live interactions. Their long-term value must be assessed when, in your career, you draw from this warehouse of situational experience. Participating in training scenarios will help you remember what you learn because you are totally engaged in the project — mind, body, sensations, and imagination. You will work hard, often without knowing you are doing so. You will come away from each simulation with a new inventory of business experience, often without realizing that you have made the acquisition.

Each scenario assigns roles, poses a dilemma, and calls for a solution. However, this is not theater. These situations have no scripts. As in everyday life, you will script your own behavior as the action unfolds. In interaction with others, you will adjust your role to changing circumstances. You will decide when to compete and when to cooperate, when to hold out and when to give in. This kind of learning requires you to think on your feet, make decisions, and be willing to accept the consequences.

Learning by *doing* does not negate *thinking*. Reliable decision making and resourceful implementation will depend on your analysis of a situation. But thinking alone does not lead to business success. You must act and *re*act in the company of others. No one in business operates in isolation. People arrive at decisions through communication. When those decisions get implemented, they call for additional interaction. Business is a corporate enterprise, not an individual activity, and it is learned best through experience.

Training scenarios are a good way to *introduce* concepts of business communication and an excellent way to *apply* concepts learned by more traditional means. This experiential approach is not useful only in the university classroom; it is also the preferred method of in-house professional training. General Motors uses training scenarios for leadership development among managers. Blue Cross and Blue Shield uses role-playing situations to teach new management trainees. The hospitality industries, from airlines to hotel management, rely on interactive training techniques. The military has long been a proponent of teaching through simulation. Aspiring lawyers learn their trial skills in moot court. Law enforcement agents anticipate life-and-death crises through training scenarios with real-action situations.

Simulation and role-playing are ways to practice living. They train the intuition as well as the intellect, the body and voice as well as the mind.

Within the relative safety of a narrative situation, they teach lessons applicable to real-world decision making. This approach acknowledges that learning is a process of becoming. Although demanding hard work, it also provides a lot of fun.

## ROLE-PLAYING BUSINESS INTERACTIONS

At first, role-playing may seem a bit awkward and even a little scary. However, you must remember that these scenarios are not public performances to entertain an audience. They are laboratory experiments to enhance your learning. They require no special skills, apart from a serious commitment to understanding workplace interactions. Everyone can take part. They encourage real-world risk taking while providing the safety net of a classroom laboratory. In a simple way, the exercise you already tried — announcing a personal decision to different people — was a simulation in which you played a role. "Practicing business" in this way means taking into the laboratory of a workplace situation the theories and principles that you have already learned and testing their validity against specific circumstances.

Simulations can be used for training and research in several areas of business operation: sales, marketing, budgeting, forecasting, transportation, and inventory, to name only a few. The primary concern here is business and organizational *communication,* a broad label including interactions in conversation, through the media, and in corporate presentations to various constituencies. The scenarios provided here involve private and public communication, one-to-one and small-group communication, face-to-face and technological communication. The human voice will be translated into print, amplified sound waves, and digital readout. The roles you will enact call for individual decision making and corporate accountability.

The everyday settings of the scenarios will give you experience with business players, organizational rules, corporate values, bargaining, negotiating, threats, bluffs, coalitions, cooperation, competition, outcomes, payoffs, solutions, gains, and losses. To play a role successfully, you will learn to interact strategically with others. You will balance change against choice, risk taking against risk management. You will calculate the probability of various outcomes for each potential action and work to reduce the level of uncertainty in a given set of circumstances.

Practicing business through workplace scenarios is a playful way to learn. Not too long ago, playfulness was taboo in corporate cultures. *Playful* was defined mistakenly as the opposite of *serious.* Now, thanks to the maverick values of entrepreneurs and the creativity of high technology, playfulness and improvisation are recognized as necessary tools for productivity in business. Innovation is a discipline of the relaxed mind and a precondition for creativity.

Each scenario has a five-part format: introduction, scene, problem, assignment, and documentation. A situation in which one or more persons are confronted with a communication dilemma is outlined. A general context and a specific conflict are described. You then analyze, enact, and resolve the situation. Each exercise concludes with a specific assignment, and your instructor will provide a deadline for its completion.

**INTRODUCTION.** The scenario begins with a title and some general background, along with a statement of learning outcomes to be achieved.

**SCENE.** This is the storyline or narrative situation. All information necessary to complete the assignment is included in this section. However, you may fill in additional details to lend plausibility to your decision making and action. The "Scene" identifies roles and setting.

**PROBLEM.** Here is a statement of the conflict embodied in the narrative scene, the communication dilemma you must resolve.

**ASSIGNMENT.** This is your specific task in the scenario, what you are expected to do. An assignment may call for writing, speaking, interviewing, or some other communication activity.

**DOCUMENTATION.** Some scenarios require printed material as part of the assignment. Such documentation is provided at the end of the format.

If a situation requires a specific reporting formula, a model is included in the scenario, usually under the heading "Strategic Planning" or "Job Appraisal." Where appropriate, worksheets are provided. Where necessary, technical information is included "FYI" (for your information).

The remainder of the book is devoted to thirty-two training scenarios. These are divided into four groups, focusing in turn on writing and reading (Part One), speaking and listening (Part Two), interviewing and small groups (Part Three), and media and technology (Part Four). This sequence, moving from simple to more complex issues, is useful, but it is not mandatory. Some classes may find it profitable to alternate among types of scenarios. Acquiring communication skills for business and organizational settings is not a one-time proposition; these skills must be practiced in various contexts. Thus the learning objectives of these scenarios overlap, reinforcing the lessons of one exercise in the demands of the next.

Training scenarios are not examinations with right and wrong answers. They are role-playing situations that require concentrated attention and lively participation. It will not take you long to enter in and feel comfortable. After engaging in each scenario, be sure to pull back and analyze the lessons you have learned.

# BUSINESS WRITING AND READING

# EXPERIENCED EXPEDITER WANTED

·············· **INTRODUCTION**

An expediter is a person who solves problems through sound judgment and quick action. Nowhere are these skills more necessary than in dealing with customers. Solving other people's problems requires looking at a situation through their eyes, adopting their vantage point. Resolving the complaint of an angry customer or an impatient client makes high demands of business communication skills. Honesty, promptness, and courtesy are of the essence if you are to save the sale, protect the negotiation, or strike the bargain. Ultimately, the aim of a business expediter is to retain a customer by solving his or her problem.

In this scenario, you will play the role of an expediter, a customer service representative. You will read four complaint letters and write responses that promise immediate attention. The exercise calls on your careful reading, your ability to take the customer's perspective, your strategic writing skills, and your quick judgment.

·············· **SCENE**

You are a college graduate with a B.A. in English literature. You live in a large city and need a job. After several weeks of pounding the pavement and following up leads, you are still empty-handed. You have looked hard without success and are now willing to consider jobs outside your major. One morning, while scouring the newspaper want ads, you read of a new position:

*You* have high energy, initiative, and intelligence. *You* possess good communication skills. *You* can type. The ad looks promising, except for the need for experience. You have certainly never been an expediter at a mail-order firm. However, throughout your entire education, you have been engaged in creative problem solving. Especially when researching and writing papers, you learned to work independently under pressure. These qualities must count as experience in expediting, you figure; so you decide to give Taurus Enterprises a call. The manager asks you to come to the office that very day for an interview and a "trial run."

That afternoon at Taurus you fill out a job application and take a tour. While talking with the manager, you pick up several important pieces of information. Taurus is a new operation, in business for just eight months. It places ads in large-circulation, slick magazines that sell unusual, high-ticket items. Taurus does not manufacture merchandise. Rather, it designs and produces ads for various manufacturers. Taurus places the ads in magazines, receives and processes all mail orders, and contacts the manufacturers for shipment to the customers.

You learn that during its eight months of operation, Taurus has been very successful at landing magazine accounts, contracting with prestigious manufacturers, and attracting customer orders. In fact, the company has already processed several thousand orders — and that is where the problem comes in. Taurus Enterprises has no customer service representative. Taurus's efforts have been so concentrated on setting up the business and negotiating contracts that customer service has received almost no attention. Letters of complaint have piled up, and no staff member has been assigned to handle them. On your tour, the office manager points through a doorway into an office where four large cardboard cartons sit on the floor. Each is brimming with unanswered customer letters, some still unopened. If you get the job, your first task will be to respond to all those complaints.

............ **PROBLEM**

After the tour, the manager tells you that getting this job will depend on your success during a trial run as customer service representative. She tells you to sit down at the desk, open the first four letters you draw out of one of the complaint boxes, and write responses for each one. Your four letters will not actually be sent. Your task is simply to read the complaints carefully, answer as you see fit with the limited knowledge you possess, and bring the completed letters to the office manager within one hour.

When you ask how you can possibly solve any customer's problem without knowing the ins and outs of Taurus Enterprises, the manager says, "Don't try to solve their problems now. What the customer needs at the moment is two things: an apology for the delay in responding to the letter and an assurance that the problem will be handled promptly. You've got to pacify the customer, hang on to the sale, and buy us a little time to sort things out."

You ask, "How am I supposed to do that?"

The manager, smiling, answers, "That's *your* problem."

## Assignment ............................................................

Write responses to the four complaint letters reprinted on pages 16–19. Follow the advice given by the office manager. Whether you compose originally at the typewriter or word processor or by hand, remember that your success will depend as much on how the finished letters *look* as on what they *say*.

---

**FYI** FYI FYI FYI FYI FYI FYI

**Lay out your business letters in a *full block* pattern with all parts set at the left margin.**

- o Address of Taurus Enterprises
- o Date
- o Address of customer
- o Salutation (Dear _____ :)
- o Body (single-spaced, with double-spacing between paragraphs)
- o Closing
- o Your signature
- o Your typed name

Russell Franklin
232 Park Avenue
New York, NY  10017

April 25, 1992

Taurus Enterprises, Inc.
800 Commercial Terrace
Los Angeles, CA  90078

To Whom It May Concern:

On February 17 of this year I placed an order for two "Antique Replica Jaguars" (Model Number 3672-3) Listed at $69.95 each as advertised in AUTO ART.  The ad promised delivery within 4 to 6 weeks.  As more time has elapsed and I have still not received my orders, please cancel immediately.

I would appreciate a confirmation of this request to cancel. Thank you for your attention to this matter.

Sincerely,

Russell Franklin

Russell Franklin

April 23, 1992


Dear Sir or Madam,

    Ordinarily I'm a patient person, but this
is getting ridiculous.  This is the third letter
I've written to you, and I've placed two phone
calls.  I have yet to receive a return letter.
On the phone, you said that my problem was being
handled.
    What's happening?
    Are you going to replace my defective tele-
vision or do I have to take this story of your
incompetence to the Better Business Bureau?
I expect a prompt answer to this letter. Make
that, I would like to receive a prompt answer.
Given your history, I can't expect anything from
you people.



Mrs. May Babcock
Rt. 4
Munice, Indiana  47302

Dear Taurus,

I have a problem, and I hope you can help me. I ordered a miniature potted spruce tree from you. When it arrived, the tree was in good condition, and I read all of the instructions for proper care. I placed the pot on top of my television set so that I could see it all the time.

Just two days later, the tree began to look sickly. It lost its vibrant green. And, after the fifth day, needles began to dry up and fall off. I thought maybe the tree was going into dormancy so I didn't call you about it. Now a month has passed, and I'm quite certain the tree has died.

As I say, the tree seemed to be in perfect condition when I received it, so I'm not blaming you. I just want to know if I did something wrong. You see, I would like to order another minia-ture spruce but am afraid that the same thing might happen to it. Could you have somebody from the tree nursery call me and answer my questions please? I'd be very grateful.

Oscar Franelli
Room 14
Rolling Acres Retirement Village
Middleton, Ohio  45042

ROBERT SCHRAM
P.O. Box 1617
Phoenix, AZ 85001

April 1, 1992

Taurus Enterprises, Inc.
800 Commercial Terrace
Los Angeles, CA 90078

Dear Mr. President:

I am angry. My son ordered genuine leather saddlebags and paid you
$489.00 from money he had earned and saved. What he received
were saddlebags of cheap imitation leather. He wrote to you twice
asking for his money back. Now I'm stepping in.

Either you send an immediate refund for the full amount of the pur-
chase, or I will instruct my attorney to file a suit against you for fraudu-
lent advertising.

I have already canceled our subscription to the magazine in which
your ads appeared and have informed the editor of my dissatisfaction.

Most sincerely,

*Robert Schram*

Robert Schram

cc: Alexander & Alexander
    Attorneys-at-Law

# TO WHOM ARE YOU SPEAKING?

·············· **INTRODUCTION**

In some circumstances, the same information may need to be presented in entirely different ways in order to communicate effectively with various audiences. For instance, you may report good news in quite different words to your spouse, to a neighbor, to an employer, to a parent, or to a competitor. In this scenario, a single piece of information must be reported to three constituencies, each with a different viewpoint and each with its own vested interest. The assignment will challenge your abilities to look at a single situation from multiple perspectives and then to adapt your writing to the needs of different audiences.

·············· **SCENE**

You are president of Ballantine Trucking, Inc. Your 450 union truckers have been on strike for higher wages for three weeks, causing a total shutdown of operations. At a meeting of the board of directors, it was decided that you should hire as many nonunion truckers as possible to keep the rigs moving for the duration of the strike. At the current rate of loss, Ballantine Trucking cannot sustain more than another few weeks of strike, yet the wage increases demanded by the union would cut deeply into corporate profits. Hence no settlement is in sight, and hiring new truckers seems the only alternative. You concur with the board's decision and agree to follow through immediately.

·············· **PROBLEM**

You need to inform three groups of the board's decision and of your action: the striking drivers, the nonstriking employees of Ballantine Trucking, and the local press. All groups require the same information (that nonunion drivers will be hired to replace striking truckers), but each one has vested interests that call for different strategies of communication.

1. Write a memorandum (see form on page 22) to all striking drivers in which you announce the plans to hire nonunion replacements for the duration of the strike. Because striking drivers may be rehired after settlement, try not to burn bridges for future negotiations.

2. Write a memorandum to the nonstriking employees of Ballantine Trucking. Announce the same information as in the first memo, trying to ensure the continued loyalty and high morale of these workers.

3. Write a press release for distribution to local newspapers, radio, and television stations in which you announce the board's decision. Try to explain your action clearly so that the local community can understand the rationale.

---

**FYI** FYI FYI FYI FYI FYI FYI
.......................................................................................................

A press release should be concise. Deciding what information to include and what to exclude is important. Use the following format as a generic guide:

Name of Organization
**For Immediate Release**
For additional information: contact

_____

**Headline**
Body of Announcement
# # #

---

4. Conduct a job appraisal (see form on page 23) of the communication effectiveness of the memos and the press release.

# MEMO

## Ballantine Trucking, Inc.

600 South Huron
Chicago, IL 60617

DATE:_____

TO: _____

FROM:_____

RE: _____

## JOB APPRAISAL   Ballantine Communiqués

**1.** If I were a striking trucker, this is what I would think of your memo, and why.

**2.** If I were a nonstriking employee of Ballantine Trucking, this is what I would think of your memo, and why.

**3.** If I were a member of the local press, this is the story I would probably report after reading your release, and why.

**4.** In what specific ways is the information in the three communiqués changed by the style of writing and the relationship implied between writer and reader?

# GHOSTWRITING 1
## Letter Composition

·············· **INTRODUCTION**

Ghostwriting is composition by one author under the name of another. A common practice at the executive echelon in corporate or political organizations, ghostwriting calls for close collaboration to merge the content, style, and viewpoint of two individuals into a single voice. Ultimately, the signature author (not the ghost) is accountable for every word, sentence, and paragraph of a document distributed under his or her name. Thus the ghostwriter is responsible for representing accurately the other's intention. In this scenario, you will work with a partner, serving alternately as ghost and as signature author of two letters.

·············· **SCENE**

Your college or university has a President's Advisory Council made up of seven students who, together, serve as a sounding board for presidential policy and decision making. Membership on the PAC is both a high privilege and a great responsibility. In the past, your president has often credited this group with sound judgment and decisive counsel. Those who serve on the PAC can make a real difference.

You have been nominated to be a representative on the PAC. Before an election is held, each nominee is asked to write a one-page letter to be published in the student newspaper. In that letter, you should spell out specific objectives and policies you would like to see addressed if you are elected to the PAC. All students will cast their ballots after reading and comparing the public letters of candidates.

·············· **PROBLEM**

You have thought through the content of your letter, narrowing the range of issues and concerns to the ones you consider most important for your campus to address this year. But when the day comes to write the letter, you are taken ill with a nasty flu bug, and there is no way you can write a coherent letter. Hence you prevail on a friend to ghostwrite your letter.

1. To enact this scenario effectively, imagine that the President's Advisory Council actually exists on your campus. Think about what specific goals, objectives, policies, and actions you would advocate if elected to serve on such a council. Do not make up issues or concerns. Use the events and problems currently confronted on your campus as the basis for your thinking. Individually and privately, decide what content you would like to include in such a letter.

2. Find a partner. You and your partner will be both ghostwriter and signature author for each other's letters. Each individual will write the other's letter. Exchange information. Participant 1 (ghostwriter) quizzes participant 2 (signature author) about what information he or she wants included and in what style or tone. During this discussion, the ghostwriter may take notes, but you and your partner may not actually compose the letter together. Your instructor will set a time limit for this conversation.

3. Reverse roles. Participant 2 (now the ghost) asks questions of participant 1 (now the signature author) about the letter he or she would like to have written.

4. Each partner ghostwrites a letter. Remember that you are representing the other person's ideas, viewpoint, and tone of voice. Type the letter that you have written, and show it to the signature author for his or her signature.

   The ghost may need to revise the writing to satisfy the signature author. The signature author should not sign until he or she is perfectly comfortable with the letter. Your instructor will provide a deadline for writing and, if necessary, revising the letter.

**To the Campus Community:**

Sincerely,

(YOUR NAME)
_____

Candidate for President's Advisory Council

# GET THE POINT?
## Creating a Pencil Ad

.............. **INTRODUCTION**

Here is a two-part sales scenario that draws on your skills in writing, graphics, and advertising. In Part One, you will create a magazine ad. In Part Two, you will become an advertising executive deciding which design, among competing entries, you should use for a new account. To enact the scenario effectively, you will need to brainstorm creative strategies for advertising a commonplace product. You will need to design and execute the ad. And you will need to judge which one, among many, will communicate most effectively to a specific magazine readership.

.............. **SCENE**

Leadbetter, Inc., is the manufacturer of ordinary lead pencils. The company has created a new line of #2 pencils to be test-marketed for college students. The pencil's three special features are (1) its shiny black finish, (2) its brand name pressed into the wood and highlighted with silver paint, and (3) its silver-colored eraser. In all other ways, this new pencil is like any other #2 pencil; it has the same length, same quality of lead, and same quality of eraser. The pencil will be marketed in retail stores for $3.60 per dozen. Leadbetter decides to hire an ad agency to name the new pencil and to design its debut ad for the college consumer. In Part One, you are that ad agency.

.............. **PROBLEM**

Your primary problem is to design a one-page ad to be placed in the back-to-school issues of several national magazines that appeal to college and university students. The challenge here is to sell such a mundane item as a lead pencil. What would motivate a college student to seek out a particular brand of lead pencil when any old #2 would probably do? Your second problem is to persuade the executives at Leadbetter to buy your design.

## PART ONE

Choose a brand name for this shiny, black Leadbetter, a name that will be pressed into every pencil in silver. Then design the one-page magazine ad. There are no restrictions on the look of your ad. It can be as simple or complex as you like; it may include graphic or verbal appeals or both. However, it cannot deviate from the product description and price provided here.

The ad proposal that you submit should contain two pages. The first is a sketch of the ad itself. (You may assume that if your ad is accepted, the final version will be produced by a professional graphic artist. Your submission is merely a sketch.) The second page should be a typed, double-spaced explanation of your advertising strategy for the ad. Explain why you think your idea will sell the product. The audience for this sales pitch is Leadbetter executives. Your task is to persuade them, through the sketch and explanation, to give you the advertising account.

## PART TWO

After all ads have been submitted, you will take on the role of a Leadbetter executive. Your instructor will display all of the proposals and invite the executives as a group to discuss their appeals and drawbacks. Then, as an individual, you will fill out a job appraisal (see page 29) to identify and explain your top three picks.

## JOB APPRAISAL    Leadbetter, Inc., Ad Campaign

Which design would you rank first among the submissions for our new product campaign, and why? (Be specific in identifying the qualities or features that should appeal to our target market.)

Which design would you rank second, and why?

Which design would you rank third, and why?

If your first choice is selected to represent Leadbetter, name two specific magazines in which you would recommend that we run the ad, and explain why these selections are appropriate.

# A CHAIN LETTER

•••••••••••••• **INTRODUCTION**

This scenario explores in-house communication by requiring a sequence of memoranda to report the same information to different people within an organization. You will call on your skills in audience analysis and memo composition. The goal of "A Chain Letter" is to introduce the variables of *hierarchy* and *power relationships* to your practice of business communication. As a piece of bad news moves up the organizational chart, each memo writer will need to balance self-interests with corporate objectives. Each link in the chain from local to regional to national level demands upward communication that acknowledges the power differentials between writers and readers.

•••••••••••••• **SCENE**

Bayfront Insurance is a comprehensive insurance company offering personal and group policies covering auto, fire, health, hospitalization, property, and life. It has local offices throughout the United States, a district office in each state, four regional headquarters in Philadelphia, Atlanta, Los Angeles, and Chicago, and corporate offices in Baltimore. At the local level, business is conducted by *sales representatives*. These men and women report to a *district sales manager*, who in turn reports to a *regional vice president*. The regional vice president reports to the *corporate vice president for sales*, who reports to the *president*.

Overall sales in the New York City office have fallen an unexpected 37 percent during the first quarter of the current fiscal year as compared with the same period a year ago. Because New York City is the single largest local office, its sales figures have historically predicted trends of growth and decline for the company nationally. Whereas such a 37 percent drop clearly represents bad news, it is not immediately apparent how serious the problem may be. Until New York's performance can be compared with the performance of other areas, and until a thorough analysis of the New York figures can reveal whether losses are widespread or isolated, there is no way of knowing the scope of the problem. If a quarterly loss of 37 percent were to point to a national trend within Bayfront, its consequences could be long term for the company as a whole and devastating to the careers of individual managers or executives.

## PROBLEM

Even before the final sales figures are tabulated and reported formally, an informal (confidential) report of the bad news must be made through corporate channels. This poses a problem that is not as simple as it may at first appear. The information to be reported is clear enough: the New York office has experienced an overall quarterly loss of 37 percent, and interpretation of that news awaits further analysis. The challenge is to report this information while still preserving relationships within the hierarchical network of the corporation.

## Assignment

### PART ONE

The assignment will be carried out by groups of five.

1. The first person in the group writes a memo as *senior sales representative* in New York City to the *district sales manager*. Report the 37 percent overall decline in sales. Remember that you are giving bad news to your boss, who will in turn carry the same information to his or her superiors. Decide the best way to report such information. This is your first year as senior sales representative in New York; hence some people in the company may be willing to pin the sales decline on you.

2. The second person in the group, acting as *district manager*, receives the first memo, reads it, and writes his or her own memo reporting the same information to the *regional vice president* in Philadelphia. Be sure to report the information clearly. Complicating the corporate relations between this writer and reader is the personal fact that they competed for the regional vice presidency two years ago.

3. The third member of the group plays the role of *regional vice president*. He or she receives the memo from the district sales manager, reads

it, and writes a memo to the *corporate vice president for sales* in Baltimore. Although this person has been regional v.p. for only two years, Bayfront's president has commented that he or she could "go all the way to the top some day."

4. The fourth member of the group must play the role of *corporate vice president,* who reads the regional vice president's memo and passes the information along in a new memo to the *president.* These two executives occupy adjoining offices at corporate headquarters.

5. The fifth member of the group, the *president,* after reading his or her memo, writes a new memo back to all the local sales representatives in New York City, expressing corporate reaction to the first news of their sales performance.

Letterhead for all of the memos is on page 34. In each case, before writing a memo, balance your reader's needs and interests against the mandate to report bad news clearly. Throughout this scenario, group members may not consult with one another. Only the single recipient of a given memo should read it. You may create additional plausible details to fill out the scene, but you may not alter the basic information that has been given.

## PART TWO

After the scenario is completed, the group as a whole should analyze the communication variables in each memo and answer the following questions:

1. After reading the first memo, speculate about the relationship between the senior sales rep in New York and the district sales manager. What specific clues does the memo offer to understanding their relationship? Look at what is said, what is not said, and how the information is presented. Pay particular attention to word choice and the sequencing of information within the memo.

2. Describe the relationship between the district sales manager and the regional vice president as coded into the second memo.

3. Describe the relationship between the regional vice president and the corporate vice president as represented in the third memo.

4. Describe the relationship between the corporate vice president and the president in the fourth memo.

5. Describe the personality and perspective of the president as evident in his or her memo to the sales representatives. Inasmuch as these men and women probably do not know the president personally, their impressions may be formed entirely on the basis of written communications such as this memo.

6. Discuss the ways in which power and hierarchy seem to influence writing strategies in this sequence of memos. Analyze the strengths and weaknesses of each link in the communication chain.

*Memorandum*

**BAYFRONT
INSURANCE**

Baltimore, Maryland

**To:**                     **Date:**

**From:**                   **Subject:**

# GHOSTWRITING 2
## Speech Composition

.............. **INTRODUCTION**

Ghost speech writing occurs frequently in the service of public officials and corporate executives. A ghostwriter's task may vary from conducting background research to editorial polishing to composition of a complete manuscript. As with ghostwriting for print, a close partnership is demanded for success. The ghostwriter attempts to represent a speaker's knowledge and viewpoint toward the subject, to reflect a speaker's personality and style in relation to the audience, and to capture a speaker's distinctive voice in his or her use of language. Ultimately, the speaker will be held responsible for every word uttered in the speech, regardless of the actual author. In this scenario, you will work with a partner, serving alternately as ghostwriter and as speaker. Your goal is to form a working relationship in which one writer can provide suitable words for another speaker.

.............. **SCENE**

You are an account executive at a large investment firm and are frequently invited to speak to civic and business organizations on the workings of the stock market. You enjoy delivering such speeches, but you do not always have time to compose them yourself. Hence you occasionally ask your assistant, a good writer, to draft your speeches.

You have been invited back to your high school to deliver a 4- to 5-minute presentation for Career Day. The topic is fairly broad: "Why Go Into Business?" Your audience will comprise high school juniors and seniors representing a wide range of academic and extracurricular interests. These are not just students from the Business Club. They come from every area of the high school program: science, literature, math, social studies, foreign languages, music, art. Your speech should reflect your own thoughts and feelings about the values of a business career (for example, social values, financial rewards, personal achievements, ethical concerns, and other motivating factors). Your remarks should be tailored to gain and hold the attention of a particular audience. How can you compel a favorable response to the question "Why go into business" from an audience of juniors and seniors in high school?

## •••••••••••••• PROBLEM

Career Day is scheduled for the Tuesday after your Sunday return from a conference in Tokyo. Because you simply do not have enough time to write this speech yourself, you ask your assistant to ghostwrite some comments that you can deliver. You have clearly in mind the themes you want to emphasize, and you need to communicate them to the assistant so that the resulting speech will be yours.

## Assignment ••••••••••••••••••••••••••••••••••••••••••••••••••••••••••••••••••••••••••••••

Work with a partner, but not the same partner as in "Ghostwriting 1." Each individual will write the other's speech. A 4- to 5-minute speech requires a manuscript of two or three double-spaced pages, no more. In the role of ghostwriter, you will conduct an interview with the speaker to learn what information, approach, and style he or she wishes to take. As writer, remember to submerge your own approach to the topic in the service of the speaker's intentions. Use his or her preferred language, structure, examples, and tone (including humor).

Reverse roles.

The class will use the form on page 37 to critique the speeches from the perspective of high school juniors and seniors at the Career Day presentation.

## JOB APPRAISAL  "Why Go Into Business?" Speech

Speaker:_____

Evaluator:_____

**1.** From the perspective of a high school junior or senior, how would you rate the speaker's vocabulary? Be specific in identifying word choices that were effective and ineffective.

**2.** How would you rate the overall tone of this speech for this audience? Particularly note the apparent attitude of the speaker toward the audience.

**3.** Identify the major persuasive appeals of the speaker (for example, personal examples, statistics, case study, historical perspective), and evaluate their communication effectiveness.

**4.** Note any specific examples of this speaker's attempt to identify with his or her audience, including humor.

**5.** Overall, identify the single greatest strength and weakness in this speech in terms of its communication effectiveness for this audience.

# A CLOSE CALL

••••••••••••• **INTRODUCTION**

College athletics take the hot seat in this scenario. The reputation of an entire university is at risk because of questionable practices by administrators of the intercollegiate athletics program. The situation is akin to a large corporation being measured by the conduct (or misconduct) of one division.

To enact this scenario, you will become a university president and decide how much responsibility to shoulder for the misdeeds of other university officials. In a position of high visibility, you will have to address the concerns of multiple constituencies under the special pressure of Homecoming festivities. At stake are the future of athletics at your university, the public reputation of the school, the financial support of alumni, future enrollments, the credibility of your administration, and perhaps, your job. The situation calls for clear thinking, keen judgment, and timely action. It will draw on personal communication skills, both verbal and written.

•••••••••••••• **SCENE**

SCU (Southeastern Commonwealth University) is a large, comprehensive, private university. It enjoys a reputation for academic excellence, athletic achievement, and high social life. SCU has a long history, dating back 150 years, and boasts many notable alumni, including persons in government, science, medicine, and the entertainment industries. You are the university president, inaugurated just two years ago. To celebrate the 150th anniversary of the school, you have planned a grand gala. Media attention is focused on SCU as the date of the public celebration approaches. Celebrity alums have been invited back to campus for special ceremonies, and a large production crew has been hired to film the festivities. The highlight of the celebration will be the November 14 Homecoming football game.

On November 6, the SCU student newspaper runs a short column on the back page announcing the unexpected resignation of assistant football coach Max Wickers. On November 7, the SCU student paper runs a two-column story reporting that Max Wickers is under investigation by the NCAA for alleged recruitment violations. You call an emergency meeting of the athletic director and coaches and learn confidentially that a recruitment scandal at SCU is about to break into the news. Incontrovertible evidence proves that under-the-table payments have been made to more than twenty scholarship football players, including the quarterback, three starting linemen, and an All-American running back. Suspicion of complicity points to the entire coaching staff and, possibly, to university officials higher up. A full-scale NCAA investigation is guaranteed with the likelihood of serious sanctions against SCU, perhaps even resulting in the loss of its football program.

.............. **PROBLEM**

With just one week before the Homecoming game and its attendant festivities, you try to anticipate and handle as many internal and external communication problems as possible. You are eager to maintain credibility without aggravating an already bad situation. You want the university community to keep this story in perspective, especially at this early stage before a full investigation.

**Assignment** .........................................................................................................

Create a presidential strategy for handling the multiple communication problems entailed in this scenario. Work through the following five-day schedule prior to Homecoming on November 14. Remember: the first time that anyone heard of this situation was the *November 6* story of an assistant coach's resignation. On *November 7*, you called a secret meeting of the coaching staff and received the bad news of the impending investigation. Begin your five-day campaign on Monday, *November 9*, just five days before the Homecoming game.

1. Write a press release, dated November 9, stating your perspective on any impending NCAA investigation. Remember: your coaches have already told you that an investigation is inevitable; however, none has been announced. This gives you an opportunity to get out ahead of the story. (See page 41 for the press release format.)

2. On Tuesday, November 10, write a 2-minute speech (one page, double-spaced) that you could deliver in the locker room before practice to the football team. Show your support for the team. Help them focus on Saturday's game without dismissing the seriousness of an impending investigation. (Page 42 shows a sample format.)

3. On Wednesday, November 11, you decide to send a memorandum to all SCU faculty on the subject of an impending NCAA investigation of the football program. Write a one-page memo stating the situation clearly and trying to keep things in perspective. Think through the special relationship that you, as college president, have with the faculty. Compose your memo by anticipating their communication needs. (A sample memo form is on page 43.)

4. On Thursday, November 12, write a guest column (250-words) for the SCU student newspaper. The column should be addressed to students and focus on their participation in the weekend's Homecoming festivities. Remind them of the university's high visibility with national press attention. (A sample form for this column is on page 44.)

5. On Friday, November 13, just one day prior to the Homecoming game, write a 250-word guest column for the town newspaper, *The Savannah Gazette*. The column should be addressed to visiting alumni, welcoming them back to campus and inviting their full participation in the Homecoming festivities. (A sample form is on page 45.)

When composing all of these communications (a press release, a speech, a memorandum, and two newspaper columns), pay special attention to the needs of each audience. Remember that as the investigation heats up, every word you speak or write will receive careful scrutiny. What you say to one constituency on one occasion will be held up for accuracy and consistency with what you say to another group on another occasion.

# PRESS ANNOUNCEMENT

**For immediate release**

**Southeastern Commonwealth University**
Savannah, Georgia 31402

November 9, 1992

For further information, contact _____, Assistant to the President
(YOUR NAME)

**(912) 555-2930**

**Southeastern
Commonwealth
University**
Savannah, Georgia 31402

November 10, 1992

**Remarks to the SCU Football Team**

By _____ (YOUR NAME)

President, Southeastern Commonwealth University

# MEMORANDUM

**Office of the President**

**Southeastern Commonwealth University**

Savannah, Georgia 31402

November 11, 1992

**To:** SCU Faculty

**From:** (YOUR NAME), President

**Subject:** _____

**Southeastern
Commonwealth
University**
Savannah, Georgia 31402

November 12, 1992

**Guest Column for** _____ SCU Student Newspaper _____

**Preferred Headline:**

_____

By _____ (YOUR NAME)

President, Southeastern Commonwealth University

**Southeastern
Commonwealth
University**
Savannah, Georgia 31402

November 13, 1992

**Guest Column for** _____ The Savannah Gazette _____

**Preferred Headline:**

_____

By _____     (YOUR NAME)

President, Southeastern Commonwealth University

# POLITICS AND PROFITS
## A Contested Policy

·············· **INTRODUCTION**

As commercial enterprises (both small and large) become more international, and as national economies (both First World and Third World) become more global, seemingly simple business decisions can have far-ranging ramifications. Ethics and politics are intimately linked with products and profits. Capital investments, labor practices, and trade policies become rallying points for groups inside and outside an industry. Often, the constituencies of a particular business have conflicting interests in its operations. Management, employees, investors, competitors, and members of the community may all look at things a little differently.

In this scenario, you will draw on your ability to look at an issue from multiple perspectives. You will work in a small group. You will need to read with sensitivity and compose with strategy. The goal is to advocate a specific policy while taking into account the conflicting viewpoints of others.

**SCENE**

American Fittings, Inc., is a manufacturer of industrial copper products, headquartered in Tucson, with mining subsidiaries throughout southeast Arizona. After its annual meeting, the board of directors issues a press release (see page 49) announcing plans to start up mining and manufacturing operations in the copper-rich Andes Mountains of Chile. The reasons for taking this step include low labor costs and large ore deposits in South America. Anticipating possible objections to the decision, the board also announces that the jobs of no current U.S. workers will be lost.

The corporate announcement by American Fittings prompts response from three important constituencies: the United Copper Workers of America, the *Daily Arizonan,* and shareholders. The United Copper Workers of America (a union), issuing its own press release, condemns the corporate decision on the economic grounds that it will inevitably lead to fewer copper jobs for union workers. Unless American Fittings reverses its decision, the UCWA threatens some kind of job action in protest.

The *Daily Arizonan* (a large-circulation newspaper) publishes an editorial against the decision of American Fittings on the political grounds that it is exploiting cheap foreign labor at the expense of American citizens.

Seventy-five shareholders of American Fittings get together and write an open letter that they sell as an advertisement in two Tucson and Phoenix newspapers. The letter applauds the decision to start up operations in Chile on the grounds of free enterprise.

## •••••••••••••• PROBLEM

These statements, pro and con, pose a major public relations problem for American Fittings. The corporation would not choose to alienate its American workers, its local communities, or its investors. No single response from executives will satisfy all three constituencies, but some kind of response is required. Management must weigh the short- and long-term consequences of all possible statements. You will first enact the role of one of the constituency groups and then give the executive response of American Fittings.

## Assignment ....................................................................

### PART ONE

Three small groups are needed for this scenario. For Part One, groups will be assigned as follows:

Group A: representatives of the United Copper Workers of America

Group B: editorial writers for the *Daily Arizonan*

Group C: concerned shareholders of American Fittings

The assignment for Group A is to write a 250-word press release from the UCWA in response to the announcement of the American Fittings board of directors. To accomplish this task, you will need to abandon whatever your personal viewpoint may be toward this situation and take on the perspective of American union representatives. Think as they would. Adopt their values. See the scene through their eyes. Write a persuasive press release, including a specific job action that you would consider an appropriate response if American Fittings carries through with its announced plans.

The assignment for Group B is to compose a 250-word editorial for the *Daily Arizonan* questioning the plans of American Fittings along the lines suggested in the "Scene." When developing your case, bear in mind the newspaper's credibility with readers.

The assignment for Group C is to write a 250-word open letter from 75 concerned shareholders that can be sold as a newspaper advertisement. Give voice to the logic of corporate profitability without ignoring fairness to employees. Do not settle for clichés. Work for a forceful presentation of your ideas.

## PART TWO

For the second part of the assignment, you will switch roles but not group. Each group will change its viewpoint as follows:

Group A: editorial writers for the *Daily Arizonan*

Group B: concerned shareholders of American Fittings

Group C: representatives of the United Copper Workers of America

Repeat Part One of the assignment from these new perspectives.

## PART THREE

Still remaining in the same group, switch perspectives once again, and write the assignment from the last remaining viewpoint.

## PART FOUR

After writing the documents called for in Parts One, Two, and Three, remain in the same group, and change your identity to become the management team of American Fittings. Assuming that you now have read the union's press release, the newspaper's editorial, and the shareholders' advertisement, write a corporate position paper (no more than three double-spaced pages) addressing the issues raised by the three constituency groups.

# American Fittings, Inc.

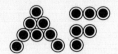

200 Enterprise Drive, Tucson, Arizona  85702

December 1, 1992

**For additional information contact**
Jack Martinez, Associate Vice President for Operations, at

**602-555-2231 (8 A.M. - 4:30 P.M.)**

## "American Fittings Goes International"

The Board of Directors of American Fittings, Inc., of Tucson, AZ, announces plans to start up mining and manufacturing operations in Chile effective the first of the year.

The decision represents corporate expansion, not retrenchment. New markets, lower costs, and increased profitability are the objectives.  No loss of jobs to American workers will result from this international expansion.

The executives of American Fittings, Inc., look forward to a good working relationship with the government and people of Chile.  To the work force of that region, American Fittings promises new jobs, fair wages, and nondiscriminatory labor practices.

# # #

# BUSINESS SPEAKING AND LISTENING

# A LANGUAGE SCAVENGER HUNT

·············· **INTRODUCTION**

The words used typically within any business can signal the attitudes, beliefs, and values of that organization. Vocabulary and manner of speech express what members believe in, are willing to reward, are likely to punish, and choose as symbols of group identity. Two tests of language usage are especially revealing. Both may be expressed as questions:

"How many synonyms does an organization employ to say the same thing?"

"What metaphor recurs most often to describe organizational values and policies?"

Sociolinguists tell us that the first question is a reliable measurement of organizational values. Members create multiple words for things that the culture values highly. According to this test, for example, American culture seems to place great stock in money because there are so many words to refer to it: *moolah, dough, bread, cash, loot,* and so on. If your class were to brainstorm, this list could be expanded to a considerable length. The American culture also provides many synonyms for *automobile, technology,* and *sexuality.* When many words exist, it is easy for members of a culture to talk about a given subject. Great value is placed on the things for which there is a large vocabulary.

The second question zeroes in on metaphor. Does a recurring metaphor in the everyday talk of organization members point to shared values, beliefs, or attitudes? Some organizational cultures describe themselves as a *team.* Others use the metaphor of *family.* Still others prefer to identify their organization as a *military unit.* These are only some of the most common metaphors. Many others exist. Such images for expressing organizational identity make a real difference to the quality of life and relationships within a given business culture.

- A *military metaphor* honors chain of command, rank, orders, and loyalty. Its marketing strategies are battle plans, and its competitors are enemies. Military language values efficiency over democracy.
- A *family metaphor* honors relatedness, kinship, seniority, security, and home. Family language values participation and congeniality over orderliness.
- A *team metaphor* honors competition, strategy, aggressiveness, play, and vigor. It yields game plans, rule books, and scorecards. Team language values winning over convention.

Monitoring language usage within an organization can be one of the prime measures of a *communication audit* carried out by a consulting team. For organizations in crisis or transition, language usage will point to significant issues of group identity, shared values, and managerial style. It can be especially helpful for resolving conflict and achieving consensus.

In this scenario, you will work as a member of an investigative team to discover and monitor the language behavior of one organizational culture, your academic department. The primary communication skill that will be required to complete your assignment is probably the hardest one to develop: good listening.

### SCENE

Working in a small group of three to seven, imagine that you are part of a team of consultants hired by your academic department to report on the department's cultural values as measured by typical language usage. By means of unobtrusive observation, interviewing, and written documents, you will need to collect data on typical language behavior of organization members. Those data will require analysis to discover any patterns of usage across the organization. Then, if possible, you may be able to draw conclusions about departmental values as measured by language usage.

### PROBLEM

Your problem is to find instances of language behavior in obvious and out-of-the-way places and then to analyze them for patterns of meaning.

1. The class is divided into five investigative teams. Team A is assigned to collect data from *department faculty*. Team B is assigned to collect data from the *department chair*. Team C is assigned to collect data from *department staff*, including clerical staff and academic adviser. Team D is assigned to collect data from *students majoring in the department*. Team E is assigned to collect data from *student organizations*. (If your department has several student organizations, you may need to assign additional teams to this part of the investigation.)

2. Meet with your team and decide the best strategy for collecting instances of language usage among your target population. All teams will need to combine opportunities for unobtrusive observation with explicit interviews. Listen particularly for (a) multiple words used to describe the same thing and (b) metaphors used to describe the department. In the latter case, you may ask for a direct description of the department in metaphoric terms — for example, "Would you describe the working relationships in this department more as those of a team, a family, a military unit, or some other analogy?" Brainstorm as many possible sources of information as you can, and do not forget formal departmental documents such as working papers, constitutions, bylaws, and minutes. In this scenario, written materials are secondary to live interaction, but they may still be helpful.

3. Team members accept individual responsibilities, trying to divide the task equitably according to time requirements and degree of difficulty. Using the sample forms on pages 56 and 57, collect synonyms and metaphors, noting the source of each. Use a separate page for each cluster of related words.

4. After all data have been collected individually, the team compiles a master list of synonyms and metaphors. Then, team members working together search for patterns or connections among the data that may point to departmental beliefs, values, attitudes, or shared identity. Notice, too, where there may be instances of conflict between incompatible uses of language.

5. The team writes a two-page, double-spaced report describing the organizational values of your department as coded into the language behavior you observed. Avoid passing judgment. Work for precise descriptions and careful analysis.

# Synonyms

Root Concept or Reference: _____

| SYNONYMS | NAME OF SPEAKER OR OTHER SOURCE | DATE |
|---|---|---|
| 1. _____ | _____ | _____ |
| 2. _____ | _____ | _____ |
| 3. _____ | _____ | _____ |
| 4. _____ | _____ | _____ |
| 5. _____ | _____ | _____ |
| 6. _____ | _____ | _____ |
| 7. _____ | _____ | _____ |
| 8. _____ | _____ | _____ |
| 9. _____ | _____ | _____ |
| 10. _____ | _____ | _____ |
| 11. _____ | _____ | _____ |
| 12. _____ | _____ | _____ |
| 13. _____ | _____ | _____ |
| 14. _____ | _____ | _____ |
| 15. _____ | _____ | _____ |
| 16. _____ | _____ | _____ |
| 17. _____ | _____ | _____ |
| 18. _____ | _____ | _____ |
| 19. _____ | _____ | _____ |
| 20. _____ | _____ | _____ |

## Organizational Metaphors

Root Metaphor: _____

| INSTANCES OF USAGE | SPEAKER OR OCCASION | DATE |
|---|---|---|
| 1. _____ | _____ | _____ |
| 2. _____ | _____ | _____ |
| 3. _____ | _____ | _____ |
| 4. _____ | _____ | _____ |
| 5. _____ | _____ | _____ |
| 6. _____ | _____ | _____ |
| 7. _____ | _____ | _____ |
| 8. _____ | _____ | _____ |
| 9. _____ | _____ | _____ |
| 10. _____ | _____ | _____ |
| 11. _____ | _____ | _____ |
| 12. _____ | _____ | _____ |
| 13. _____ | _____ | _____ |
| 14. _____ | _____ | _____ |
| 15. _____ | _____ | _____ |
| 16. _____ | _____ | _____ |
| 17. _____ | _____ | _____ |
| 18. _____ | _____ | _____ |
| 19. _____ | _____ | _____ |
| 20. _____ | _____ | _____ |

# HOSPITAL-ITY
## A Two-Party Negotiation

••••••••••••• **INTRODUCTION**

This scenario takes place in the health-care industry, an enterprise located on the threshold between public service and business. Health care is expensive. Everyone needs it, but not all can pay for it and some health-care providers cannot afford to donate their services. Therein lies a personal dilemma for physicians and, in the long term, a societal dilemma for national policy makers.

For this scenario, you will work in a group of three. Each group will engage in a two-party negotiation, with the third member observing the process. In order to resolve the policy problem presented in the "Scene," you will need to practice good listening, logical thinking, persuasive speaking, and constructive compromise. The scenario will conclude with a short written document.

•••••••••••••• **SCENE**

Two physicians decide to resign their positions in the emergency room of a local hospital, where they have worked together for many years, and form their own emergency clinic. The clinic will be a privately owned facility, and the two founding partners will be principal shareholders. Their desire to found a new emergency-care clinic springs from their dissatisfaction with the quality of medical care and the fiscal inefficiency of the hospital's services. They are convinced that their facility will provide better care, at comparable cost to the patient and greater profit to the physicians. Almost all of the planning and logistics for this joint venture have been worked out: financing, staffing, and physical plant. With the opening date only six weeks away, the two physicians get together one evening to discuss one final matter of policy: "What stance will our clinic take toward the treatment of indigent patients?"

○ Federal and state law require that any licensed emergency-care facility *must* provide treatment to patients in life-threatening circumstances *regardless of the patient's ability to pay.*

○ In non-life-threatening situations, an emergency-care facility may decline to accept patients without the ability to pay.

Despite being old friends and sharing a good working relationship, the two physicians know that this particular issue may be the cause of considerable dispute between them. They have never agreed on the obligations of a medical facility to provide routine treatment to patients without insurance or other means of payment.

The two physicians meet one evening in the relaxed atmosphere of one of their homes to sort out their differences on this issue and to write a short policy statement about the care of indigents, a document they can both endorse with confidence.

## PROBLEM

Dr. A advocates that their emergency-care clinic should not treat any patient in a non-life-threatening situation who does not possess the means to pay (for example, cash or insurance). Dr. A's reasoning is based on the profitability of their corporate venture. Dr. B believes that emergency care should be offered to all patients under all circumstances regardless of their ability to pay. This rationale derives from the Hippocratic Oath pledging a physician's services to all in medical need.

## Assignment

1. One member of the group plays Dr. A, and one plays Dr. B. The role-players need not personally agree with the positions espoused by their characters. In fact, it may be more interesting and challenging to play a position opposite to the one you personally hold. Much can be learned from adopting a perspective quite different from your own. The third member of the group will serve as a silent observer of the interaction.

2. Prior to engaging in this two-party discussion, each role-player should start by analyzing his or her own perspective and preparing for negotiation. To assist in your preparations, separate worksheets are provided for Dr. A and Dr. B (see pages 61 and 62).

3. After preparing individually, the two role-players should meet to formulate their corporate policy on indigent care. The third group member will observe. During the discussion, the role-players may not recognize or interact with the observer.

4. Continue the discussion until both Dr. A and Dr. B can agree on a position. Then Dr. A and Dr. B together write a single-paragraph policy describing the care to be provided in the new clinic for indigent patients in non-life-threatening circumstances. A sample form is provided on page 63.

5. After the dramatic enactment, the observer should fill out the job appraisal on page 64, describing the interaction.

## STRATEGIC PLANNING **1** Developing a Character Profile for Dr. A

**1.** Create a plausible description of Dr. A's age, gender, and background, given the circumstances described in the "Scene." Summarize Dr. A's character in one well-developed paragraph.

**2.** Summarize Dr. A's position toward the care of indigent patients in non-life-threatening circumstances. Writing as Dr. A, articulate a rationale for the clinic's valuing profits over the care of certain patients. Use the first-person pronoun *I*.

**3.** Without violating Dr. A's basic position, under what non-life-threatening circumstances, if any, would Dr. A consider admitting a patient for emergency care who did not show the means to pay?

**4.** Predicting that Dr. B does not share Dr. A's views, outline the points of probable disagreement on which Dr. A may be willing to compromise and those points about which Dr. A insists on holding firm.

## STRATEGIC PLANNING **2** Developing a Character Profile for Dr. B

**1.** Create a plausible description of Dr. B's age, gender, and background, given the circumstances described in the "Scene." Summarize Dr. B's character in one well-developed paragraph.

**2.** Summarize Dr. B's position toward the care of indigent patients. Writing as Dr. B, articulate a rationale for the clinic's valuing patient care over profitability. Use the first-person pronoun *I*.

**3.** Without violating Dr. B's basic position, under what circumstances, if any, would Dr. B consider refusing a patient for emergency care who did not show the means to pay?

**4.** Predicting that Dr. A does not share Dr. B's views on open admittance, outline the points of probable disagreement on which Dr. B may be willing to compromise and those points about which Dr. B insists on holding firm.

## Policy
## Governing
## Patient Admittance

Date _____

Signature of Dr. A _____

Signature of Dr. B _____

## JOB APPRAISAL   Admittance Policy Negotiation

1. Summarize your first impressions of Dr. A at the beginning of the meeting. From the character's appearance, behavior, and speech, what level of confidence and what apparent attitudes did the physician display? Support your conclusions with specific observations from the discussion.

2. Answer the same question about your first impressions of Dr. B.

3. Outline the position presented by Dr. A. What arguments of support did he or she present?

4. Outline the position presented by Dr. B.

5. State the points of specific conflict between the two physicians.

6. By what strategies of negotiation did the two physicians try to resolve their conflicts?

7. Does their written policy statement accurately reflect the resolution of this conflict?

# COMPUTER GAME
# SALES CONFERENCE

### INTRODUCTION
Here is a sales scenario drawing on your public communication skills. In it, you will play two roles: entrepreneur and investor. The assignment calls for creative thinking, audience analysis, presentational performance, and fiscal judgment. Specifically, you will need to make a 5-minute oral presentation with visual aids. And, in your role as investor, you will need to listen critically to a sales conference of other presentations, deciding how best to invest a limited amount of capital. The communication goals of the scenario are to develop effective sales strategies and, more abstractly, to observe the connections between presentational skills and consumer psychology. What could motivate a group of potential investors to lay out capital in support of your idea? The venue for competition is computer games.

### SCENE
Techno-Fun is an investment firm bringing entrepreneurs in the maverick industry of computer games together with speculative investors. Annually, the firm holds a private sales conference at which new, small companies may pitch their innovative ideas for computer games to a select audience of potential shareholders. The conference is charged with the excitement of high risk. For those who are selling, the conference represents an opportunity to attract needed capital and, thus, to move an idea from the drawing table into the marketplace. For those who are buying, the conference represents an opportunity to get in on the ground floor of a potentially highly profitable new company. For both seller and buyer, the negative risks are as great as the positive ones. There is the real possibility that a new idea for a computer game will not win investor confidence or that a major capital outlay will not yield an acceptable return. You will play both roles — entrepreneur presenting a new game and investor in the proposal of others.

As entrepreneur, you will need to make a 5-minute oral presentation at the Techno-Fun sales conference. Then you will play the role of potential investor for all other presentations. Remember: as entrepreneur, you are not selling a product to consumers; rather, you are selling an *idea* to potential investors.

When preparing the presentation, you will need to anticipate the knowledge, analyze the needs, and predict the concerns of your audience of potential shareholders. Careful investors will need to be persuaded of the viability of your idea. At the same time, they must feel confidence in you as a manager (that is, in your sound judgment, your market analysis, your energy and drive, your ability to deliver on your promises). Ultimately, an investor will need to be convinced that a commitment of capital to your company will yield a profitable return.

## Assignment .........................................................................................

### PART ONE

Your first role is computer game entrepreneur. Name the company and create an idea for a marketable new computer game. Market research and brainstorming will be required. Do not settle for the first thing that comes to mind, but generate a long list of possibilities. Yours could be an adaptation of an existing nonvideo game (for example, a sport or board game). It could be a computer representation of a television or film adventure. It could be an educational game. It could derive entirely from your imagination. (You may not sell a new edition of a computer game that already exists.) As with any creative development of a new product, secrecy is important. Beware of industrial spies.

After deciding on a computer game, determine a strategy for displaying your idea in a 5-minute oral presentation. What kinds of questions do members of your audience need answered before making a commitment? How much do they already know about the computer game market? What is the best way to move them from games with which they are familiar to the product you are proposing? Try to supply all the information necessary to arouse investor interest and to overcome predictable resistance. Because you are a new company trying to attract initial investments, you may not rely on a track record of past sales to validate your promises. Instead, you will need to rely solely on the idea itself and your speculative research into its market potential. Your 5 minutes offer a no-holds-barred challenge to attract investors against the competition of other, equally motivated, entrepreneurs. The only rule constraining your presentation is the 5-minute time limit, which will be strictly enforced.

In making the actual presentation, you may use media, graphics, handouts, or other aids to public communication. Remember that the presentation should be compelling at the moment of delivery and memorable after the fact. Give the audience something to remember you by when it comes time to make their investment decisions. Persuasive appeal depends on (1) the plausibility of your idea, (2) the feasibility of your market analysis, (3) the communicative power of your presentation, and (4) the long-term memorability of your arguments.

## PART TWO

Your second role in this scenario is that of investor. When sitting in the audience for the sales conference, you need to think and act as a potential investor willing to put capital into a new idea. Listen carefully to each presentation and apply the rigorous standards of investor skepticism required to test an idea for soundness and profitability. Remember that your judgment will cost you money. You dare not base investment decisions on popularity or equality. Invest in the presentations that you think will fly as corporate ventures in the highly competitive market of computer games.

After all presentations have been made, you may fill out a stock order form (see page 68), purchasing a total of fifty shares of stock. Assume that share prices are equal across all presentations. You may not invest in your own company. You could invest fifty shares in one presentation, twenty-five in each of two, ten in five, five in ten, and so on. Your instructor will collect the stock order forms and tabulate results.

This sales conference is a formal occasion requiring proper attire and demeanor from both presenters and audience. Presentations should meet professional standards of verbal and visual communication.

# Stock Order Purchase Form

DATE: _____     SIGNATURE: _____

PRINT NAME: _____

**COMPANY/PRODUCT NAME**            **SHARES PURCHASED**

1.                                  _____

2.                                  _____

3.                                  _____

4.                                  _____

5.                                  _____

6.                                  _____

7.                                  _____

8.                                  _____

9.                                  _____

10.                                 _____

**TOTAL: 50 SHARES**

# DEBATE 1
# Educational Philosophy

············· **INTRODUCTION**

A debate is a time-honored forum for the rational exchange of conflicting ideas. Debating takes place in legislatures, courtrooms, and board meetings. It requires solid reasoning, good supporting evidence, and a careful matching of one side's arguments against opposing viewpoints. Debate formalizes the turn taking of everyday conversation. The interaction between debaters depends on good listening as they assert and defend, make their points and counterpoints. Whether on the affirmative or negative side of a question, whether delivering a set speech or an improvised rebuttal, expert debaters display concentration and reasoned strategy in their efforts to communicate clearly and persuasively.

Although it seems that the purpose of a debate is to persuade others, in business or government the purpose may be quite different. A formal debate separates issues by setting up one position in clear contrast to another. The result can be clarified thinking on both sides and can lead, ultimately, to creative compromise.

In this scenario, you will work with a partner, preparing and executing a modified formal debate. The assignment will call on your skills in research, rational thinking, organization, and verbal presentation. During the actual debate, attentive listening will pose a special challenge.

············· **SCENE**

Imagine yourself as a business professional, commercially successful and respected in the community. At a meeting of the board of higher education in your state capital, you have been invited to address this question, "Should the baccalaureate degree focus on pre-professional training or on a general background in the sciences, arts, and humanities?" The board is considering curricular reform and resource allocation for its state universities. Hence the members want to see the alternatives clearly before making recommendations. They have already had input from educators. Now they turn to you, representatives of the business community, for your considered opinion. After hearing the debate between pre-professional and liberal arts approaches argued forcefully, the board may decide to advocate one or the other stance. More likely, it will strike a balance between the two perspectives. To achieve a proper mix, the board turns to debate as a means of separating out the issues.

## •••••••••••••• PROBLEM

This scenario asks you to present a compelling case in favor of either pre-professional training or liberal arts instruction as the preferred focus for higher education. If you take the stand that undergraduate education ought to be pre-professional training, your problem will be to argue that a curriculum should be geared specifically to the on-the-job demands of various professions. The problem for advocates of the opposite argument, that a liberal arts background is preferable, is to claim that exposure to great thinkers, artists, and theorists of the past will prepare a graduate to enter any specific profession and to adapt to changing circumstances.

To debate the issue, you will need to build a case based on your own experience and reasoning. Draw, too, from the published opinions of recognized authorities as reported in current books, periodicals, and newspapers. (*The Chronicle of Higher Education* is a good resource.) In order to persuade board members of the validity of either perspective, you will need to present a convincing case for your position as well as attack the deficiencies of the opposing side. You might not be assigned to advocate the position you personally hold on this issue. Try to construct a compelling case for whichever side you are given.

## Assignment ...........................................................................................

One two-person team defends the pre-professional viewpoint, and another two-person team presents the liberal arts position. On the day of the debate, speeches should follow this format:

| | |
|---|---|
| Pre-professional viewpoint (first presenter) | 5-minute speech |
| Liberal arts viewpoint (first presenter) | 5-minute speech |
| Pre-professional viewpoint (second presenter) | 5-minute speech |
| Liberal arts viewpoint (second presenter) | 5-minute speech |

| | |
|---|---|
| Pre-professional viewpoint (first presenter) | 3-minute rebuttal |
| Liberal arts viewpoint (first presenter) | 3-minute rebuttal |
| Pre-professional viewpoint (second presenter) | 3-minute rebuttal |
| Liberal arts viewpoint (second presenter) | 3-minute rebuttal |

The first-round speeches (5 minutes each) may be prepared in advance. The second-round rebuttals should be 3-minute extemporaneous speeches responding specifically to the reasoning and evidence presented in the first round.

The audience for the debates uses the job analysis sheet provided on page 72. Remember that debates, like boxing matches, are scored on the basis of contact (that is, assertion and refutation).

## JOB APPRAISAL   Focus on the Baccalaureate Degree

**1.** Summarize the case presented in support of the pre-professional, job-training position.

  o *Case:*

  o *Major arguments:*

  o *Supporting evidence:*

  o *Line of reasoning:*

**2.** Summarize the case presented in support of the liberal arts position.

  o *Case:*

  o *Major arguments:*

  o *Supporting evidence:*

  o *Line of reasoning:*

**3.** Analyze the strength of rebuttal presented by the pre-professional debate team. Be specific in citing points of contact in refuting the opposing case.

**4.** Analyze the strength of rebuttal presented by the liberal arts debate team. Be specific in citing points of contact in refuting the opposing case.

**5.** If you were a member of the board of higher education, on the sole basis of the cases presented in this debate, which curricular orientation (pre-professional or liberal arts) would seem more sound to you? Why? Be specific in referring to the comparative advantages you now see in the two models of higher education.

# "IT'S MY PARTY"
## A Case of Mistaken Identity

**INTRODUCTION**

This scenario poses a management problem requiring diplomacy. It begins with a simple misunderstanding, escalates quickly, and could end, depending on how you handle it, in significant personal and corporate embarrassment. As in so many circumstances faced by business executives, diplomatic intervention may be critical to resolving or containing this volatile situation. You will work individually. The situation calls for quick thinking, damage control, and one-to-one communication with several people.

·············· **SCENE**

You are manager of the prestigious Los Angeles Ratcliffe Hotel owned by Harrison Ratcliffe, renowned for his close ties to United States presidents and his generous financial support of the Republican Party. The Republican National Committee is scheduled to meet in Los Angeles to plan strategy for upcoming campaigns. The meeting is not the presidential nominating convention, but it is a newsworthy event and many national reporters are in town to cover it. Deborah Braden, chair of the Republican National Committee, will be staying as a guest of the hotel in the Presidential Suite on the top floor. In fact, the Los Angeles Ratcliffe is providing free rooms to several high-ranking party officers, all on the hotel's top floor and all as legitimate gifts of Mr. Ratcliffe. These arrangements were made many months in advance of the February meeting.

In November, three months before the event, a Gerald Vines phones the hotel and requests booking for the days when the Republican meetings will be in town. He specifically asks whether the Presidential Suite is available. The reservations clerk checks and says, "No, but I could put you in the Eisenhower Suite just one floor below." This suits Mr. Vines, and the reservation is confirmed.

Two days prior to the arrival of both Mr. Vines and Ms. Braden, you receive a furious phone call from the hotel's owner, Mr. Ratcliffe: *"What* have you done? Have you lost your mind? Booking the chairman of the Democratic Party into my hotel when I'm hosting Deborah Braden! Are you trying to make me look like the world's biggest fool or what?"

This is the first you have heard of the problem. In fact, you cannot believe that it is true. "Wait a minute, Mr. Ratcliffe," you say. "I can't believe we've booked Vines. And if we have, I was never informed."

"Well, I hope you haven't booked him, for *your* sake."

"Where did you hear such a thing?"

"Where did I *hear* it?" Mr. Ratcliffe shouts into the phone. "I just got off the line with the President of the United States, who wanted to know if this was some kind of joke. Vines ran into Braden at a Washington restaurant last night and said he would be seeing her at the Ratcliffe this weekend."

"I'm sure there's been some kind of mistake, Mr. Ratcliffe," you assure your boss. "But, even in the event that we did book both party chairs, I don't think it would be a catastrophe."

"You don't, eh?"

"No, sir."

"Well, let me clue you in on a thing or two. When I invite my special friends to stay at the Ratcliffe, I'm not in the habit of hosting the opposition party at the same time."

"But, sir, you didn't . . ."

"Don't 'but sir' me. If Vines and Braden are both booked into my hotel this weekend, and I have to find out about it from the President of the United States, I'll be the laughingstock of the Republican Party."

"Now, Mr. Ratcliffe . . ."

"And that *will* be a catastrophe, I can tell you. And do you know why?"

"No, sir. Why?"

"Because, among other things, I'll have to start looking for a new manager for the Los Angeles Ratcliffe, that's why."

The next thing you hear is a loud click on the line. End of conversation.

After this phone call, you start right into action, going first to the reservations desk. Sure enough, Gerald Vines, chair of the Democratic Party, is booked into the Eisenhower Suite. When you seek out the clerk who took the reservation, he says, quite innocently, "How was I to know who Gerald Vines was? Nobody told me I shouldn't take a reservation from any Gerald Vines. I thought you'd be pleased that I booked the Eisenhower for this weekend, what with the Presidential Suite gone as a freebie."

The next thing you do is place a call to Democratic National Headquarters in Washington, D.C., and ask for Gerald Vines. His secretary says that he is not in. You explain that you are the manager of the Los Angeles Ratcliffe and that a rather embarrassing situation has come up. "It seems that we've booked Mr. Vines for a suite at the same time that we will be hosting Ms. Braden. We wouldn't want to cause any embarrassment or discomfort to either guest, so, if it's all right with Mr. Vines, I believe I can get him the penthouse at the Palisades. We will be happy to pick up the tab in appreciation for any inconvenience this may cause Mr. Vines."

The secretary answers, "I don't think that will be necessary, thank you. Mr. Vines specifically wanted to stay in your hotel and is very pleased at the prospect of occupying the Eisenhower Suite. He has a confirmed reservation, I believe, and is looking forward to arrival on Friday. Thank you for thinking of him, however. I'm sure he won't be the slightest bit embarrassed to be sharing the Ratcliffe with Republican leadership."

"I don't believe you quite understand the situation," you say, trying to remain calm.

"Oh, I understand perfectly. Perhaps Ms. Braden's party would care to switch hotels."

You conclude, "No, I think not."

## PROBLEM

You have arrived at an impasse. Here is the situation in summary. Inadvertently, your hotel has booked the chairs of both the Republican and the Democratic parties for the weekend of the Republican National Committee meeting. This has angered the hotel's owner, your boss, and could escalate into a thoroughly embarrassing situation for you and the Los Angeles Ratcliffe. In the worse-case scenario, you can envision this thing exploding into a media side show with Harrison Ratcliffe depicted as a buffoon. What options are available to resolve your dilemma, or, at least, limit its potential PR damage?

## Assignment

### PART ONE

You keep a confidential journal in your office in which you often scribble thoughts, recollections, or plans. Write an entry in which you analyze this situation, spelling out as many options as you can conceive and then devising a plan of action. You are not writing with the thought that anyone else will read the journal. This is simply a way of clearing your brain and trying to bring some order to a chaotic situation. Specifically, determine how you will address the following problems:

1. What communication, if any, would be appropriate or advantageous with Mr. Vines? (Remember, you have spoken only to his secretary so far.)

2. What communication, if any, would be appropriate or advantageous with Ms. Braden?

3. What will you say next to Mr. Ratcliffe, and how will you say it?

4. What communication may be required with the hotel staff in this situation?

5. Under what circumstances, if any, might you need to communicate with the press? If necessary, what approach will you take?

**PART TWO**

After enacting the plan devised in Part One, imagine that you receive another phone call from Mr. Ratcliffe wanting an update on the situation. On the form on page 77, write the telephone dialogue verbatim as you think it might take place when you explain your actions to your boss. Try to take on both roles, imagining a plausible conversation representing your own perspective and that of Mr. Ratcliffe. (You may want to return to "Scene" for hints on the creation of a telephone dialogue.)

# Telephone Transcript

Call placed by Mr. Harrison Ratcliffe to

Mr./Ms. _____

Los Angeles      February 14, 199__

Speaker's Name                        Dialogue

_____    _____

_____    _____

_____    _____

_____    _____

_____    _____

_____    _____

_____    _____

_____    _____

_____    _____

_____    _____

_____    _____

_____    _____

_____    _____

_____    _____

# DEBATE 2
# Management Cross-Examination

············· **INTRODUCTION**

Cross-examination debate allows participants to question one another, challenging or defending their options and evidence under close scrutiny. In this scenario, you will debate the advantages and disadvantages of three different management philosophies. The task calls for separating out variables that are ordinarily intertwined in the daily decision making of corporate executives. The purpose of this debate is *not* to determine a winner or loser. It is to create a forum for the clear discussion of differing philosophies.

············· **SCENE**

Groups of three are invited to debate the following question: "To whom is a corporate CEO most accountable when making major decisions?" One group member will be assigned to defend one of the following three answers: (1) the shareholder, (2) the employee, (3) the customer. You are all experienced CEOs and will conduct your debate before a management seminar in an MBA program.

Almost every major decision made by a CEO takes into consideration all three constituencies. Ultimately, what is good for investors is probably good for employees and customers as well. Likewise, what is good for customers should be advantageous to employees and shareholders, and what is good for workers should benefit consumers and investors. Nevertheless, however much they may overlap, the interests of these three groups are not identical. In order to explore subtle distinctions among managerial approaches, this scenario asks you to rank-order the accountabilities of executive decision making. As CEO, to whom are you *most* accountable: shareholders, employees, or customers? Or, to put it another way, which of these three constituencies do you think of *first* when making major corporate decisions?

**PROBLEM**

You will be assigned to defend one of the three positions, regardless of your own personal management philosophy. Your problem is to muster a compelling case in support of your assigned viewpoint. You may draw on real-life cases, create hypothetical examples, or quote management theories to substantiate your position. It may be especially useful to imagine situations in which the vested interests of shareholders, employees, and customers are in conflict and priorities among them must be assigned.

## Assignment ...............................................................................................

1. Your instructor will assign a position for each group member to represent.

2. The debate will proceed according to the following format:

| | |
|---|---|
| First speaker, representing shareholders | 5-minute speech |
| Second speaker, representing employees | 5-minute speech |
| Third speaker, representing customers | 5-minute speech |

After these 15 minutes of formal presentations, each group member is allowed 5 additional minutes to cross-examine the other two positions, asking specific questions about the arguments advanced, the evidence presented, or the logic used. If time permits, another segment of 15 minutes may be reserved for audience members to ask questions of the three presenters. On page 80 is a job appraisal form that may be used by audience members or your instructor to evaluate the debate.

## JOB APPRAISAL   CEO Accountability

**1.** Summarize the case presented in support of shareholders.

- ○ *Case:*

- ○ *Major arguments:*

- ○ *Supporting evidence:*

- ○ *Line of reasoning:*

**2.** Summarize the case presented in support of employees.

- ○ *Case:*

- ○ *Major arguments:*

- ○ *Supporting evidence:*

- ○ *Line of reasoning:*

**3.** Summarize the case presented in support of customers.

- ○ *Case:*

- ○ *Major arguments:*

- ○ *Supporting evidence:*

- ○ *Line of reasoning:*

**4.** Describe the points in question and clarification sought during cross-examination.

**5.** Was one position advocated more convincingly than the others? On what basis were you persuaded?

# UP IN SMOKE
## A Three-Party Negotiation

·············· **INTRODUCTION**

The rights of smokers versus the rights of nonsmokers have created a workplace controversy that mirrors a persistent debate in the society at large. Medical research continues to discover new hazards related to secondary smoke that, in turn, further motivate those who would ban smoking altogether from the work environment. Most businesses have tried to accommodate both smoking and nonsmoking employees by designating areas for their exclusive use. In some cases, however, this solution has failed to satisfy all members of the organization. Nonsmokers may feel that *any* smoking on the premises is potentially injurious to their health. Smokers, if totally denied the right to smoke, may feel that their rights have been unfairly subjugated to the demands of others. Rash statements and counterattacks may ensue. The resulting climate of accusation and defensiveness in the workplace is unhealthy for all.

In this scenario, you will enact the viewpoints of various concerned parties in a smoking dispute. A creative solution to the dilemma calls for your sensitive listening, ethical judgment, and careful use of language. The goal is to act decisively in your managerial role while preserving a sense of community in the workplace. Communication skills are always tested when balancing the rights of an individual against the values of a group.

·············· **SCENE**

Livingstone Engineering employs a total of forty-five people. Most of the engineers work in private offices, as do the president and vice president. The drafting room, however, is an open facility with up to a dozen persons working at drawing tables in close proximity to one another. Likewise, the clerical staff occupies a large room subdivided by shoulder-high partitions. Livingstone employees are encouraged to think of themselves as a family. Fairness, common sense, and kinship have long been the values that guided policy and practice in this professional setting.

Several years ago, when smoking became a workplace issue, Livingstone was one of the first businesses to set a policy protecting the rights of both smokers and nonsmokers. Employees with private offices were allowed to smoke in their offices with the doors closed. No smoking was allowed in the drafting room or in the clerical workers' cubicles. However, one section of the company lunchroom was set aside for smokers, and smoke breaks could be taken every two hours there. Smoking was also permitted outside: in the parking lot, on a second-floor balcony, and on the lunchroom patio. These regulations seemed to satisfy all concerned with the issue of smoking at Livingstone. From time to time, a nonsmoking word processor might grumble about the smell coming from an engineer's office, or a smoker might complain about needing to get up from the drafting table and go elsewhere to have some puffs. But, by and large, the policy seemed to work.

Enter Chris Fitzpatrick, new vice president of Livingstone. Brought in with impressive engineering credentials and accompanied by several new accounts, Fitzpatrick is clearly being groomed to take over the company's presidency on the retirement of founder A. F. Livingstone. Fitzpatrick is a high-powered, no-nonsense individual, driven by hard work and driving others to excellence. Fitzpatrick smokes incessantly. Most of the time, Chris remembers to close the office door when smoking and not to light up in the nonsmoking areas of the building. However, given the fast pace of Fitzpatrick's workday, some slip-ups are inevitable. When reminded of the company smoking policy, Fitzpatrick always, "Oh, right. Sorry."

Livingstone nonsmokers are getting irritated. Company smokers, noticing Fitzpatrick's example, are becoming a little more vocal in objecting to old restrictions. After several weeks of grumbling by both sides, a petition is circulated among the nonsmokers, asking the company president to intercede and tighten the nonsmoking regulations. At a minimum, they want the existing policies to be strictly enforced. However, they also respectfully request the implementation of more stringent guidelines that would prevent smoking anywhere in the building. Twenty-seven of Livingstone's forty-five employees sign this petition. In response, a second petition is circulated among smokers. The six signers of this appeal claim that they are being harassed by nonsmoking coworkers, and they demand the right to exercise their choice freely. Specifically, they want to see the drafting room and clerical cubicles divided in such a way as to permit smoking on the job. After all, engineers with private offices already enjoy this privilege.

The head word processor presents the nonsmokers' petition to A. F. Livingstone in the president's office. Chris Fitzpatrick, while refusing to sign the smokers' petition ("No skin off my nose"), is asked to present the thing to Livingstone. "Sure," Fitzpatrick says, winking. "I'll take it over to the boss. It's the least I can do." This is said in the company lunchroom, and

Fitzpatrick presents the smokers' petition to the president then and there, in everyone's presence.

•••••••••••••• **PROBLEM**

A. F. Livingstone has never before been confronted with employee petitions. This way of dealing with a problem certainly does not feel like the "family" thing to do. In these circumstances, the president must decide how (or if) to honor the rights of a minority of employees against the petition of the majority. In resolving the specific dilemma of the smoking policy, Livingstone wants to reduce the level of tension among employees that the issue has engendered. The president decides to call one representative from each petitioning group into the office to try to discuss the issues and reach some fair resolution.

**Assignment** ....................................................................................................

The class is divided into groups of four. Within each group one person represents the *smokers' viewpoint*, a second represents the *nonsmokers' viewpoint*, a third plays *A. F. Livingstone*, and the fourth is an *observer*. After taking time to prepare, each group enacts the scene in A. F. Livingstone's office. No formal speeches will be given, as in a debate. Simply, Livingstone should convene a meeting in which each side is invited to present its case in open discussion.

If you are one of the petitioners, try to present the most compelling arguments you can to support your viewpoint. (You need not personally agree with the position you represent in order to do a fair job of defending it.) If you are Livingstone, try to listen for points of possible compromise between the two cases presented. Ultimately, you will have to resolve the conflict by issuing a new policy statement (see the form on page 84) in response to the petitioning smokers and nonsmokers. The observer will critique the interactions occurring among the three principals (see the form on page 85).

**Livingstone Engineering**

## MEMORANDUM

**TO:**     All Employees

**FROM:**     A. F. Livingstone

**RE:**     Smoking Regulations

**JOB APPRAISAL**    Livingstone Engineering's
Smoking Regulations

**1.** Summarize the initial position and supporting arguments of the nonsmokers' representative.

**2.** Summarize the initial position and supporting arguments of the smokers' representative.

**3.** Describe the listening behaviors of A. F. Livingstone during the initial interaction. By what specific signs could you tell the president was attending to the two cases?

**4.** What resolution to these conflicting viewpoints, if any, seemed to emerge by the end of the meeting? How did this occur? Be specific.

**5.** Did the name of Chris Fitzpatrick come up in the discussion? If so, what impact did it seem to have on the participants and their interaction?

**6.** Having been privy to this interaction, and after reading the memo written by A. F. Livingstone to spell out a smoking policy, what response do you predict the new policy will have on the overall level of tension in the company?

## PART THREE

# INTERVIEWING AND SMALL GROUPS

# JOB INTERVIEW 1
## "Meet the Management"

············· **INTRODUCTION**

This scenario is a kind of round-robin job interview enacted in small groups. It requires a résumé. In switching roles between interviewer and interviewee, you will be expected to listen attentively, speak effectively, and adapt creatively to each new set of circumstances.

---

**FYI    FYI    FYI    FYI    FYI    FYI    FYI**

A *résumé* is a "summing up." In business, it represents a summing up of an individual's professional credentials.

A synonym for *résumé*, preferred in academic institutions, is *curriculum vitae* (Latin for "course of life").

A *dossier* is the complete file of a job applicant's supporting documents, including letter of application, résumé, letters of reference, and any other personnel documents.

---

············· **SCENE**

You are a job applicant for an entry-level management position in a multinational corporation, one sufficiently large and diversified to accommodate all the different professional interests of your group members. After an initial interview in the personnel office, you have been asked to meet for 10 minutes with a management team that will go over your résumé and get acquainted with your background. The purpose of the group interview is to probe your qualifications, to get a clear picture of your educational training, and to measure your ambition.

**PROBLEM**

From the job applicant's perspective, the problem of this scenario is to present a clear and detailed résumé and to explicate it in the oral setting of an interview. From the interviewers' perspective, the problem is to probe each applicant's résumé and, by asking questions, to find out exactly what the background, training, and ambition of the candidate may be.

**Assignment** ••••••••••••••••••••••••••••••••••••••••••••••••••••••••••••••••••••
••••••••••••••••••••••••••••••••••••••••••••••••••••••••••••••••••••••••••••••••••

1. Each group member should prepare a résumé summarizing his or her background. The format shown on page 93, with its word-and-phrase composition, allows for easy scanning. The format shown on page 94, written in paragraphs, allows for explanation of experience. You may use one of these formats or another format specified by your instructor. Bring enough photocopies to the interview to present one to each committee member.

---

**FYI** FYI FYI FYI FYI FYI FYI

Before beginning to write your actual résumé, create a working inventory of your interests and achievements. From these, you may select the items that are best suited to the résumé. On scratch paper, jot down answers to the following questions:

1. What formal degrees have you earned?
2. What specific job training have you received?
3. What is your military record, if any?
4. What kinds of work experience have you had?
5. What special achievements, awards, or recognition have you received?
6. What community activities and projects have you participated in?
7. What are your personal interests and hobbies?
8. What specific job skills do you possess?
9. What communication skills do you possess, including fluency in foreign or computer languages?
10. Who would be able and willing to serve as references to document your qualifications?

---

**2.** On the day of the interviews, each group should have its own space. When you are the interviewee, you will present a copy of your résumé to each member of the management panel. After reading it over, the interviewers will ask you questions specifically related to the information that it contains. When you are a panelist, try to probe for additional information about an applicant's previous employment, educational training, and job aspirations. Do not settle for generalizations; ask specific questions that invite concrete answers.

---

**FYI** FYI FYI FYI FYI FYI FYI

**Here is a list of fifteen frequently asked questions during any kind of employment interview.**

1. What makes you interested in this job?
2. What do you know about our company generally or this job specifically?
3. Why did you choose your major in college? Of what benefit could it be in this job?
4. Do you have plans for future education?
5. Which previous job, among those listed on your résumé, did you enjoy most, and why? Which least?
6. How well would you say you work with others?
7. What experience have you had supervising others?
8. What specific qualifications do you possess that might predict your success in this job?
9. Tell me an instance in which you have learned something "the hard way" on the job.
10. How would you state your professional goals?
11. Where do you see yourself in five years? Ten years?
12. Do you enjoy travel?
13. Given the choice, do you prefer to work on projects by yourself or in a group with others?
14. In what ways have you grown in your present job, or through your education?
15. Do you have any questions?

Federal law prohibits an employer from asking questions not directly related to job requirements. Here is a list of inappropriate questions that may *not* be asked either on an application form or during an employment interview.

1. What is your age? (unless age is a stipulation of employment, as in selling alcoholic beverages)
2. What is your religious affiliation?
3. What political party do you belong to?
4. What is your marital status?
5. What clubs do you belong to?
6. What is your national origin?
7. What is your maiden name?
8. What is your height or weight?
9. Are you a homeowner?
10. Do you own a car? (unless ownership of a car is a job stipulation)

**Applicant's Full Name**
Applicant's Address
Applicant's Telephone Number

## Education

19___              Most recent degree, Major, Institution

19___              Previous degree, Major, Institution

## Work Experience

19___ – 19___      Current (or most recent) job title, Organization,
                   Location

19___ – 19___      Previous job title, Organization, Location

19___ – 19___      Earlier employment, Organization, Location

## Technical Training

19___              Any in-service or other technical training

## Special Achievements

19___              Awards and recognitions  [Date and list
                   individually.]

[Other categories might include the following: **Military Service, Volunteer and Community Service, Memberships in Professional Associations, Interests and Hobbies,** and **References**.]

**Applicant's Full Name**
Applicant's Address
Applicant's Telephone Number

**Career Objective**

    Describe in one or two complete sentences your professional goals. Do so by indicating a general area of interest, not a specific job title.

**Work Experience**

    Describe your work experience in a brief paragraph summarizing each job you have held. Be sure to note major areas of responsibility and any special accomplishments. Use *italics* or <u>underscoring</u> to set off key words.

**Education**

    Describe your education, including degrees or diplomas attained. Summarize the value of your particular major to your career objective.

**Skills**

    Describe your special skills and aptitudes that are likely to match up with job requirements. Highlight technical and communication skills.

**References** (optional)

    List the names, addresses, telephone numbers, and professional relationships of colleagues or authorities *who have agreed* to recommend your qualifications.

[Other categories may be added.]

# JOB INTERVIEW 2
## One-on-One

•••••••••••••• **INTRODUCTION**

Working in a small group, as you did for "Job Interview 1," in this scenario you will gain practice in designing and answering hypothetical questions during a job interview. The special skills called for here are improvisation, thinking on your feet, and responding under pressure.

Many job interviews include at least one hypothetical situation (that is, a question that places the applicant in a set of imaginary circumstances with an implicit or explicit problem to solve). By hearing an interviewee talk through his or her response to the hypothetical situation, an employer can get some indication of a candidate's judgment and ability to handle on-the-job problems.

Hypothetical questions are mini-scenarios. They may call for technical solutions, management strategy, interpersonal skill, negotiating, or ethical discernment. Hypothetical questions are meant to put the candidate on the spot; they are meant to be difficult. However, a good hypothetical question, like a good scenario, does not suggest only one possible answer. It carries no hidden agenda. Rather, it is open-ended, testing the creative intelligence of the candidate.

•••••••••••••• **SCENE**

In this scenario, you will take on the roles of interviewer and interviewee alternately in a series of 4- to 5-minute interviews. Each interaction between employer and applicant will center exclusively on hypothetical questions. You may assume that this is *not* the candidate's first interview; thus no time needs to be spent on introductory conversation or discussion of a résumé. Also, because class members may represent different business backgrounds and aspirations, the hypothetical questions you devise should deal specifically with matters of business communication, management, or corporate ethics — subjects that cut across all business contexts. Here is an example.

Imagine that you are an administrative assistant to our sales manager, who is preparing an important quarterly report for oral presentation at a board meeting. Your boss comes into your office and says, "The West Coast office hasn't submitted their monthly figures yet, but I just talked to them on the phone and they say they're up about 5 percent over last month. Write me up a report, would you, and dummy up some figures to represent a 5 percent increase. Just sign it for Jeffries on the West Coast. He's authorized it." How would you respond?

Again, a hypothetical question is a kind of one-on-one verbal scenario. Unlike a closed interview question that asks for information, or an open question that invites discussion, a hypothetical situation reveals character and values. When asked a hypothetical question, you should feel free to take your time in answering. Think it through, and be sure of your reasons for advocating a certain response. Do not waste effort in second-guessing what the interviewer wants to hear. Tell him or her what you think, and why.

·············· **PROBLEM**

In this scenario, you will play both interviewer and job applicant. For the first role, you should prepare at least four hypothetical questions. For the second role, you will be asked to improvise answers on the spot. Challenge other role-players with the choices posed by real-world dilemmas.

**Assignment** ·································································
·······················

1. Before the class meets, devise four hypothetical questions to ask in your role as interviewer. While making them challenging and innovative, do not overcomplicate the details. Provide concrete information when setting up your situation so that the job applicant can enter into the problem's context. Establish a clear problem to be solved in business communication, management, or ethics. Before settling on the final dimensions of any hypothetical question, imagine how *you* would answer it. Be sure that you have devised an open-ended situation that calls for judgment, action, and justification. A good hypothetical situation does not demand a single best answer or rationale. It does not aim to trick the interviewee. Instead, it invites thoughtfulness and creative problem solving.

2. As job applicant, you will need to listen carefully to each hypothetical situation, ask questions as necessary to clarify the given circumstances, and offer a considered answer based on your best judgment. Let the interviewer hear the rationale behind your thinking. Take your time, and do not hesitate to lay out alternative solutions before selecting the one you would enact if presented with the actual situation.

## STRATEGIC PLANNING
### Developing a Hypothetical Question

Hypothetical questions are based on the premise *what if*. In designing yours, you may use the following questions as a checklist of circumstances to include.

**1.** "*What if* you were this kind of **person** . . ."
Decide the individual role your interviewee will play in the hypothetical question. You may give the person a name, title, or job description.

**2.** "*What if* you worked in this kind of **organization** . . ."
Describe the business in which your character works. You may name it, describe its size or location, and summarize its objectives.

**3.** "*What if* you found yourself faced with this **situation** . . ."
Lay out the circumstances of the problem. Be specific and concrete. Try to avoid guiding the interviewee along certain courses of action. Rather, stick to the facts.

**4.** "*What if,* in that situation, you were called on to **act** . . ."
Specify the dilemma to be resolved. This may take the form of a decision to be rendered, a question to be answered, a problem to be solved, or a choice to be made. Be sure that the dilemma remains firmly rooted in the circumstances of your hypothetical situation. Avoid generalizing beyond those circumstances.

These questions address the major components of a dramatic enactment: character, setting, plot, and action. The success of your hypothetical questions depends on the care with which you devise their details. *Answering* hypothetical questions calls for improvisation. *Asking* them calls for planning. In the actual interview situation, it is best to pose a hypothetical question conversationally. When preparing, though, it can be helpful to write out your hypothetical situations verbatim in order to double-check their effectiveness.

Write out each of your four hypothetical questions. Be sure that none takes longer than 1 minute to ask. Aim for 30 seconds.

# JOB NEGOTIATION
## High-Risk Interviews

............ **INTRODUCTION**

A midcareer change often necessitates high-risk interviews in which the comparative advantages of two job possibilities are weighed against one another. The risk comes into play when you measure the known qualities of a present position against the unknown probabilities of a future situation. When bargaining between two prospective employers, you may risk the loss of both positions. Metaphors such as "crossing the Rubicon," "burning your bridges," "the bottom line," and "negotiating by ultimatum" come to mind with such interactions.

In this scenario, you will enact a sequence of high-risk interviews surrounding a career move. The communication goals are (1) to enter into a negotiating process and (2) to analyze the strategies used by all participants in accomplishing their individual agendas.

............ **SCENE**

The principal players in this corporate drama are Chesterton, president of Allied Communications (a management consulting firm); Brown, president of Brown and Associates (a competing firm in the same city); and Okawa, a promising young executive with Allied. Okawa has been with Allied Communications for five years, earns a salary of $75,000 per year, and has experienced a steady pattern of professional development from project assistant to handling major accounts. Everything in Okawa's experience with Allied points to an eventual partnership in the firm, perhaps within the next five to eight years. Brown, of Brown and Associates, offers Okawa an immediate partnership at a salary of $85,000 per year.

To complicate this otherwise straightforward decision, imagine that Okawa prefers to stay with Allied because it is the more prestigious firm, better established, with bigger clients. However, Okawa wants badly to become a partner in some reputable consulting firm; hence the Brown offer has obvious appeals. Okawa feels ready to become a partner of Allied now. Chesterton does not agree. Chesterton's view is that Okawa is coming along nicely and will be a good candidate for partnership at some unspecified future date. As a final narrative twist, assume that Okawa's spouse (not a participant in these negotiations) is primarily interested in the highest possible salary and the most secure position.

### PROBLEM

Okawa enters into separate discussions with Chesterton and Brown. Okawa's preferred outcome would be to use the Brown offer as leverage to achieve partner status with Allied. Chesterton's agenda in negotiation is to keep Okawa as a loyal employee without yielding unduly on the issue of salary and without yielding at all on the timetable for a partnership. Brown's agenda is to get Okawa on board at any price.

## Assignment

### PART ONE

The class is divided into groups of three. Students are given the roles of Okawa, Chesterton, and Brown. Each participant uses his or her own first name. Starting with the narrative details provided in "Scene" and "Problem," each participant begins by filling out an imagined profile of his or her character (see the planning sheet on page 101).

No specifications are suggested for how the series of interviews should be conducted or how many may be required to reach resolution. The only two requirements are that the initial interview, in which Brown makes the offer, be between Okawa and Brown. Whether that offer is oral or written may be a point of negotiation. The second interview should be between Okawa and Chesterton. Beyond those initial two meetings, participants can shuttle back and forth as many times as necessary to reach a satisfactory resolution. At no time may all three participants meet together or be allowed to overhear one another's interviews.

The person playing Chesterton will have to decide how far he or she is willing to go to keep Okawa without violating the given circumstances of the "Scene." Likewise, the person playing Brown will have to decide how far he or she is willing to go to get Okawa. Okawa, stuck in the middle, should negotiate circumstances to his or her greatest advantage without overstepping realities or risking an unanticipated loss.

## PART TWO

After the interviews have been concluded and a resolution has been reached, all three participants in the group may engage in discussion to analyze the negotiating process and communication strategies used by each to accomplish his or her agenda. An appraisal form is provided on page 102 to assist in this discussion.

## STRATEGIC PLANNING  Developing a Character Profile

Before entering the oral negotiations of this scenario, work toward the fullest possible understanding of your character. To that end, answer the following questions.

**1.** What does my character want *most* in these negotiations?

**2.** How far is my character willing to go to get what he or she wants? Be specific.

**3.** What is my character *not* willing to give in order to achieve his or her objective? Be specific.

**4.** What other desires, besides those listed in question 1, motivate my character's interactions and decisions? List in descending order of importance.

**5.** What additional variables, other than those detailed in the scenario, might be brought into play in this negotiation?

**6.** What is my character's overall strategy in approaching these discussions?

**7.** What one image or metaphor describes my character's communicator style as he or she anticipates the negotiations?

## JOB APPRAISAL   Allied/Brown Negotiations

As a group, and no longer in character, assess the communication strengths and weaknesses of each participant in these negotiations.

1. Summarize the flow of information from one interview to the next by listing the main points of negotiation in their chronology.

2. Discuss any discrepancies of information or perception that may arise among the three participants' versions of events.

3. Discuss the areas of strength and points of weakness in the negotiating position of Chesterton. Address both Chesterton's corporate power and personal persuasiveness.

4. Discuss the areas of strength and points of weakness in the negotiating position of Brown. Address both Brown's corporate power and personal persuasiveness.

5. Discuss the strategy of Okawa in sequencing the interviews between two competing employers.

6. Invite each role-player to reveal what unused options he or she *might have considered* if the right circumstances had presented themselves.

7. In hindsight, and after discussing the experience, how might each character have changed his or her approach to these negotiations in order to alter their outcome? ("Outcome" includes changed attitudes and relationships among the participants, as well as the possibility of a job change for Okawa.)

# EXIT INTERVIEW

············· **INTRODUCTION**

Exit interviews are designed to bring meaningful closure to a process or a relationship. In a business organization, an exit interview is usually conducted when an employee leaves, whether because of retirement, resignation, or disability. The term *exit* does not necessarily connote an end to all future relations, but it does mark a decided change in the relationship. The purpose of this kind of interview is to give an organization the chance to learn something about itself from a candid appraisal by a departing employee.

---

**FYI** FYI FYI FYI FYI FYI FYI

The exit interview in this scenario assumes that a person is leaving the organization to seek a better opportunity elsewhere. Other situations that require exit interviews in a business setting may include the following:

○ Retirement
○ Disability or extended leave
○ Lay-off
○ Transfer within the organization

Notice that most of these situations represent a *changed* relationship with the organization. Discussion might focus on information that the departing employee needs, such as about benefits, insurance, and means of future contact between the organization and the individual.

In this scenario, you will have a chance to play both the interviewer and the interviewee in an exit interview. The purpose of the scenario is to focus on the special interaction required in this situation. The key term is *focus*.

## SCENE

Imagine that you have decided to leave your college or university. Perhaps your intention is to work for a while and return to school at some later date. Or perhaps you have chosen to transfer to another institution. Maybe you have received a job offer that is too attractive to pass up. Maybe personal circumstances demand that you leave school. In an exit interview with a representative from Student Services, you will be asked to respond candidly to questions about your experience in the organization (that is, at your college or university). You will have opportunity in this scenario to play both interviewer and interviewee.

## PROBLEM

As interviewer, your problem is to devise questions that probe a departing student's experiences at the institution without infringing on his or her privacy. You need to be alert to any lesson that the college or university might learn for future organizational change and improvement. At the same time, you have a public relations function to serve. Try to provide an interpersonal environment in which a positive exchange may take place. Good listening and impartiality are essential to your role.

As interviewee, your first problem is to imagine a plausible explanation for departure. Your second challenge is to reflect on and articulate your experiences as an organization member (that is, as a student in your college or university). Although the scenario calls for you to imagine a fictional choice and an alternative vision for your immediate future, your answers to questions should reflect your real experience as an organization member.

An exit interview can easily degenerate into a gripe session full of accusations and defensiveness. Or, equally unproductive, an exit interview may avoid substantive discussion and merely gloss over subjects of real importance. The interview can be stressful as the organization elicits information about itself, trying to listen carefully, and as the individual expresses his or her experience, trying to speak reflectively.

## Assignment

1. The class is divided into two groups. During one session, Group A will serve as interviewers and Group B as interviewees. In a second session, the roles will be reversed.

2. The interviewer should come prepared with an agenda of direct questions, both primary and follow-up. (See the planning sheet on page 106.) The interviewee should prepare by imagining the exact circumstances and rationale under which he or she has decided to leave the institution. Also, the interviewee should reflect on the positive and negative experiences of membership in the college or university community. (See the planning sheet on page 107.)

   The organizational interviewer needs to learn why the person is leaving. Does the departure represent dissatisfaction? If so, is the irritant widespread within the organization or localized to this person's individual experience? Most importantly, the organizational interviewer needs to design questions that can elicit an accurate and complete appraisal of the department member's experience within the organization. A good exit interview should survey both positive and negative attitudes. This blend is difficult to achieve when feelings run high at critical moments in personal and professional transition.

3. When playing the role of interviewer, you have an additional assignment. After conducting the interview, write a brief descriptive report of the interviewee's experience. (Avoid evaluation or judgment.) Present the report to the interviewee for inspection and, if the report is agreeable, ask for a confirming signature. (See the sample format on page 108.)

## STRATEGIC PLANNING **1** Developing Interviewer's Questions

You may choose to sequence your questions as follows:

1. Create questions to identify the interviewee's **role** within the college or university (for example, his or her year, major, membership in clubs).

2. Create questions to solicit the interviewee's **positive experiences** in the college or university. Try to elicit specific, rather than general, responses. Consider educational, cocurricular, athletic, social, and community-related experiences.

3. Create questions to solicit the interviewee's **negative experiences** in the college or university. Seek specific answers.

4. Create questions to characterize the interviewee's **quality of life** while in the college or university. These questions move from the concrete experiences of questions 2 and 3 to a higher level of abstraction.

5. Create questions to solicit the interviewee's **recommendations for change or improvement** in the college or university.

6. Create **open-ended questions** that allow the interviewee to say what is on his or her mind.

## STRATEGIC PLANNING **2** Developing Interviewee's Profile

In preparing for your exit interview, you may use the following guidelines as aids in recounting your college or university experience:

**1.** Create a plausible explanation for your decision to leave the college or university.

**2.** What motivated you to attend this college or university in the first place?

**3.** What activities, events, and relationships have particularly satisfied or pleased you in your college experience?

**4.** What activities, events, and relationships have disappointed you in your college experience?

**5.** What recommendations for positive change in the institution could you make to improve the quality of life for future students?

**6.** What might you have changed in your own experience to take fuller advantage of your membership in this college or university community?

## EXIT
### Interview

| Interviewer: | |
| Interviewee: | |
| Date: | |

**Reason for Leaving:**

1. Detail the interviewee's positive experiences and attitudes. Be concrete and specific. Where possible, use the interviewee's own language.

2. Detail the interviewee's negative experiences and attitudes. Be concrete and specific. Where possible, use the interviewee's own language.

3. What specific recommendations for organizational change does the interviewee suggest?

4. Describe the interviewee's overall attitude toward his or her affiliation with this college or university. Give specific support from the interview.

I have read and approved this summary of my exit interview.

**Signed:** _____ **Date:** _____
Interviewee's Signature

# AFFIRMATIVE INACTION

.............. **INTRODUCTION**
Affirmative Action and Equal Employment Opportunity provide guidelines to safeguard fair access to employment in the American labor market.
These initiatives particularly help to protect women and minorities from
discrimination in hiring and promotion. Government regulators monitor
organizational compliance; clear violations run the risk of civil penalties,
large fines, and professional censure. Yet despite legislative mandate and
societal commitment to the principles of affirmative action and equal
opportunity, abuses persist. In this scenario, you will deal with a specific
instance of institutional abuse and try to rectify the problem while mini-
mizing the damage. The situation calls for keen managerial judgment,
consensus building within an executive team, and effective communication
(both written and oral) with multiple business constituencies.

.............. **SCENE**
Whitman Technologies, Inc., is a midsize corporation specializing in the
design of environmentally safe packaging for food products. Only five
years old, the company has been touted both by conservationists and by
food retailers as a model achievement in new-wave development. It is
highly profitable, structurally lean, and youth oriented. Its president and
founder, 34-year-old Stephen Whitman, has been the subject of cover
stories in several national magazines.

In generous media coverage, Whitman has been held up as a model
of the new American industrialist. One of the exemplary policies for which
Whitman has been praised is the hiring into executive positions of several
women and racial minorities. Because of the high visibility of his fully
integrated management team, Whitman has played the public role of
champion for women's issues and civil rights. Given all this positive

publicity for its president and founder, Whitman Technologies has enjoyed a privileged status with the media. No company effort has been made to separate the public visibility of Stephen Whitman from the corporate image of Whitman Technologies. The two seem inextricably linked together.

One person who has been less than enthusiastic about Stephen Whitman is George Searls, head of personnel for Whitman Technologies. Although Searls has been partially credited for the liberal hiring policies of the company, he knows that considerable effort has been made actually to *prevent* women and minorities from receiving entry-level and midmanagement positions. For five years, Searls complied with Whitman's wishes to keep the number of women and minorities to an absolute minimum, and to limit them to low-level positions. However, he took several opportunities to complain about this policy to Whitman himself. Searls's concern was always laughed off with such comments as, "Don't you read the papers? We have more girls and blacks than anybody. We're the damned American dream. Don't go messing things up for yourself." Finally, Searls complained about the company's hiring policies at an executive meeting.

The next day, he was called into Whitman's office privately and told, in no uncertain terms, that he had better start following the company line on hiring and stop complaining. Searls, having anticipated that this would be Whitman's response, had wired himself and secretly recorded the conversation. After the one-on-one meeting, Searls resigned his position at Whitman Technologies.

## PROBLEM

The day after quitting, Searls went public with his accusation against Stephen Whitman, sending copies of his tape recording, along with a typed transcript, to several major newspapers. (See page 112 for a transcript of the damaging conversation.) Searls accused Whitman Technologies of (1) deliberately circumventing Affirmative Action and Equal Employment Opportunity guidelines in the hiring and promotion of women and minorities and (2) hiring token women and minorities into highly visible management positions to mask the company's true personnel policies.

After authenticating the tape recording as being Stephen Whitman's voice, several newspapers carry the story prominently, either on the front page or as a feature article in the business section. In response to this negative publicity, Stephen Whitman announces an immediate leave-of-absence for himself, promising, in a written statement, that "company management will be turned over completely to my able management team, which, I remind you, includes women and minorities."

## PART ONE

Working in a group of five to seven, you will become a member of Whitman Technology's management team. The group writes a report in four parts describing management's consensus about how to handle the multiple communication problems entailed in this scenario. Part 1 of the report should specify and discuss *communication problems* that you perceive in this situation. Consider the special communication needs of employees, the press, shareholders, and other interested constituencies. Part 2 should outline the various *alternatives* presented by group members as possible solutions to the problems in Part 1. A rationale for each solution should be included. Part 3 describes a *strategy of implementation* representing a consensus management viewpoint. Part 4 includes copies of all *documentation* that may be required in implementing the management policy (for example, correspondence, press releases, speeches, and transcripts of consultations or telephone conversations).

## PART TWO

Each group member should write a two-page, double-spaced report describing and analyzing the group process in the interactions described above. Identify each member's role in fulfilling the group's task. Analyze group effectiveness in arriving at a consensus management policy.

---

**FYI**  FYI  FYI  FYI  FYI  FYI  FYI
......................................................................

**Members of small groups may take on three kinds of roles:**

- *Task roles* contribute directly to achieving the group's objectives. They include initiator, information seeker, information giver, researcher, opinion seeker, opinion giver, clarifier, summarizer, and logistics manager.
- *Maintenance roles* enable an effective group process and ensure cohesion. They include energizer, supporter, gatekeeper, harmonizer, compromiser, tension reliever, and active listener.
- *Negative roles* impede progress on a task or inhibit group process. They include blocker, attacker, dominator, boaster, joker, special-interest pleader, and withdrawer.

## Transcript of Stephen Whitman
## Speaking to George Searls in Private Meeting

**Date:**      June 14, 1992
**Location:**  Whitman Technologies, Inc.
               Corporate Headquarters, Office of the President
**Tape:**      072-143


**Whitman:**  Apparently, George, you haven't grasped the big picture yet.

**Searls:**   Why don't you tell me about it.

**Whitman:**  You were pushing me yesterday in that executive meeting, and I won't
              have it.

**Searls:**   I was pushing you because I can't get satisfaction any other way.

**Whitman:**  Okay, one more time, here it is.  Just so there will be no more mistaking
              my intention on this hiring thing.  All right?

**Searls**:   All right.

**Whitman:**  We've got more than our quota of blacks and women in upper
              management. I'm all for them, and you know it.  The problem comes in
              getting too many of those types in the rank and file.  Understand?

**Searls:**   But Affirmative Action . . .

**Whitman:**  Affirmative Action be damned.  I want factory and supervisory positions
              going to real workers—not your women  and minorities.  Got it?

**Searls:**   Got it.

**Whitman**:  Well, I suggest you start considering who pays your check, George, and
              think about following orders from now on like a good company man.
              We've been together too long to mess things up now. Listen, I won't
              be crossed again in an executive meeting.  You understand me?

# THE CASE OF INFECTIOUS RESEARCH

·············· **INTRODUCTION**

Questions of academic and industrial honesty surround this scenario, with high-stakes blackmail as a real threat. A management team of three executives must make difficult decisions under great time pressure while they are spotlighted by the media.

To resolve the management dilemmas involved in this situation, you will work in a group of three. You will have to exercise ethical accountability, corporate damage control, and good public relations. Written and oral communication will be required with individuals in-house and outside the company, as well as with various media. Specifically, the decisions you make and the way you communicate them will determine the future of your corporation, this in response to a situation that blind-sides you with its unexpected circumstances.

·············· **SCENE**

Medtech, Inc., is a young corporation devoted to the research, design, and manufacture of new technologies for the health-care industries. In the company's second year, one of its star researchers discovers a chemical formula for producing synthetic blood, a significant scientific breakthrough with immediate commercial applications. The management of Medtech decides to invest all available capital in the manufacture and marketing of this product, expecting windfall profits.

The company's plan, calculated in secret meetings of its three top executives, gets an enormous boost when it goes public by receiving an unexpected award, the prestigious Franklin Medal for Outstanding Achievement, presented by the American Science Foundation in recognition of the development of synthetic blood. The medal is given to Medtech as a company and to its young researcher, Michael Milton. News of the award comes to Medtech on November 7. *The New York Times* carries the story on page 3 of its November 8 issue. Phone calls of congratulations come into Medtech from far and wide, including requests (all accepted) to write cover stories on the company and its discovery in *Time, Scientific American, Science* magazine, *The Atlantic*, and other magazines of national and international repute.

·············· **PROBLEM**

On November 9, Medtech receives a letter (see page 116) from Dr. Charles Williamson claiming that the formula for synthetic blood attributed to Michael Milton is, in fact, Williamson's formula and that Milton stole it while he was a research assistant in Williamson's lab. Williamson demands immediate satisfaction for his right of ownership.

In response to the letter, your executive team meets and calls in Michael Milton to confront him with the accusation made in the letter. He confesses his unequivocal guilt. In light of these two circumstances (that is, the letter and the confession), how will you communicate with the American Science Foundation, Charles Williamson, *The New York Times*, the magazines contracted for cover stories, shareholders, and other interested constituencies?

# Assignment ································································································

## PART ONE

The class is divided into groups of three, representing the executive team of Medtech, Inc. Discuss the managerial and communication problems you face and how you intend to resolve them. Report your deliberations in a four-part document, as follows:

1. **Communication Problems.** Identify and describe each communication problem that you see in this situation. Do not batch the problems together, but enumerate each individually. Include all possible constituencies impacted by the circumstances. For example, how will you handle Michael Milton? How will you respond to Charles Williamson? What will you say to the American Science Foundation? What will you tell *The New York Times*? What about shareholders? Employees? Customers? Other media?

2. **Alternative Solutions.** Identify all the possible solutions discussed by your management team in response to each problem enumerated above. Include a brief rationale in support of each solution. The rationales should be keyed to the communication problems — for

example, for problem 1, the management team discussed three possible solutions: a, b, c.

3.  **Strategies of Implementation.**  Identify which solution among the alternatives listed was chosen to resolve each communication problem. State why this set of solutions won consensus among the managers. When possible, work toward unanimous agreement; otherwise, rely on a majority vote and include a statement describing the dissenting rationale.

4.  **Documentation.**  Attach copies of all correspondence and any other documentation required to implement your management strategies. Include copies of in-house and public communications. If telephone calls or press conferences are part of your strategy, include verbatim transcripts of the dialogue. For correspondence, memoranda, or press releases, include copies of final drafts conforming to professional standards of format and appearance.

**PART TWO**

During the days of this scenario, each individual should keep a private journal describing and analyzing the group process of decision making. Identify the roles played by each group member in fulfilling the task. Evaluate the group's effectiveness in arriving at a consensus policy.

# WASHINGTON INSTITUTE OF TECHNOLOGY

### SEVERNA PARK, MARYLAND 21146

November 7, 1992


Chief Executive Officer
Medtech, Inc.
P.O. Box 1400
College Park, MD  20742

Dear Sir or Madam:

   From 1989 through 1991, Mr. Michael Milton was a research
assistant in my laboratory at Washington Institute of Technology.  The
formula for synthetic blood attributed to Michael Milton, and for which
Medtech has just received the Franklin Medal, was developed by me
in 1989.  I have ample proof that will stand up in court substantiating
my claim to the formula.  I can also substantiate Mr. Milton's access to
all of my research files during the time of his assistantship in my lab.

   I cannot allow you to reap enormous commercial profits from my
scientific discovery.  You have two choices: either negotiate my rights
to the formula, guaranteeing a 50 percent royalty on all sales, or see
your fraud exposed in the press.  I shall expect to hear from you in one
week.

Sincerely,

*Charles Williamson*

Charles Williamson, Ph.D., M.D.

# HELPING HANDS
## A Community Trust

.............. **INTRODUCTION**

Helping Hands is a community organization for collecting and distributing charitable contributions to local, nonprofit service projects (for example, youth centers, drug rehab programs, meals for shut-ins, aid to the homeless). Its board of directors consists of community leaders given the mandate to fund programs without consideration of race, religion, political affiliation, or corporate patronage. The awarding of funds is to be based on the sole criterion of a well-managed organization responding to a real need. In this scenario, you will be a member of a community advocacy group trying to develop a service project worthy of support from Helping Hands.

.............. **SCENE**

The budget committee of Helping Hands has $10,000 of uncommitted monies to invest in one or more new community projects for the current fiscal year. Various groups are competing for grants of $2,000, $5,000, or $10,000 from that total pool in support of their individual service projects.

Assume that the scene is your own college town or neighborhood. Given local needs, describe the service offered by your group, demonstrate the need for the service, and try to persuade the budget committee of your suitability to administer the project. The budget committee will have to be convinced that a need exists, that you have the proper remedy for meeting that need, and that yours is the right group to manage the service project. As trustees of community funds, the budget committee must be very careful to avoid supporting any program of marginal value or under dubious management. When committing the available resources, the budget committee may choose to support five small ($2,000) proposals, two midsize ($5,000) proposals, or one large ($10,000) proposal.

.............. **PROBLEM**

The decision of the budget committee will be made on the basis of 15-minute oral presentations by each group. You may, if you choose, supplement the oral presentation with written documentation. Remember: persuasiveness depends on what you say and on how you say it.

## Assignment

1. The class is divided into small groups. Each group decides on an area of need for community service. One way to make this determination is to think of a needy constituency that is not being adequately served by existing programs. Identifying this constituency will require research.

2. Each group devises a 15-minute oral presentation for the budget committee. Remember your obligations to demonstrate a need, to present a plan for meeting that need, and to represent a creditable management for administering the project. For the presentation itself, use whatever strategies of persuasion seem most appropriate and most likely to succeed. Each member of your group may choose to speak, or one representative may do all the talking. You could bring in community witnesses to support your proposal. You might need visual aids to assist the oral presentation. You may choose to distribute printed documentation of your oral proposal. Whatever the strategies devised, you may not use more than 15 minutes.

3. Before making the presentation, fill out the required proposal application form (see page 119).

4. Make the presentation in a closed session of the budget committee. Your instructor, along with two other members brought in from outside the class, will comprise the committee.

5. You will be informed in writing of the committee's decision (see the sample form on page 120).

## Helping Hands Project Application

**Give to Budget Committee before oral presentation.**

1. Names of applicants: _____

   _____

   _____

   _____

   _____

2. Title of proposal: _____

3. Constituency to be served: _____

4. Amount requested: _____

5. Briefly describe the need for your proposal:

6. Briefly describe how your proposal would meet that need:

# Report of the Helping Hands Budget Committee

**Title of Proposal:** _____

**Date of Presentation:** _____

**Amount Requested:** _____

**Recommended Funding:** _____

1.  If full funding is recommended, give supporting rationale. What features of this proposal seemed especially persuasive, given the purposes of Helping Hands? Are there any reservations or restrictions on funding?

2.  If partial funding is recommended, give supporting rationale. What features of this proposal made it worthy of funding? Why does the reduced amount seem appropriate?

3.  If the proposal is not recommended for funding, give supporting rationale. What weaknesses in the proposal itself or in its presentation led to the committee's decision? Would you recommend that the group resubmit a revised proposal at some future date? If so, what suggestions would you make?

# A SWEET DEAL TURNED SOUR
## A Problem for the
## Graff Candy Company

············· **INTRODUCTION**

An essential phase of problem solving, prior to considering possible solutions, is to analyze the problem itself. In many cases, this analysis involves studying what circumstances led to the problem (past), where things stand at the moment (present), and what may be the likely outcomes of various actions (future). In this scenario, you will work in a small group to investigate a problem between a business organization and its host community, and then you will present your recommendations in written form.

············· **SCENE**

The Graff Candy Company, founded in 1957 by Alice Graff, is a family-owned business. Located in Middleton, Iowa, the company produces, under private label, high-quality chocolates for specialty shops throughout the United States and Canada. Although Graff is a relatively small company, its payroll of seventy full-time and fifteen part-time employees has a substantial economic impact on the community of Middleton (population 8,000). Alice Graff, a self-made, strong-willed, and fair-minded person, has always been a silent supporter of the Middleton community, especially the town's youth. Beginning in 1967, 2 percent of the company's annual profits have been returned to the community in the form of yearly monetary gifts to Middleton's youth programs. These gifts have always been strictly anonymous, channeled through the Middleton Business Association, a nonprofit civic organization whose membership represents business leaders in the Middleton community (see page 124). Ms. Graff has always made it perfectly clear that under no circumstances should the identity of her company's gifts be revealed.

This scenario was designed by Dr. Mary Pelias, Southern Illinois University at Carbondale.

In 1979, Graff initiated an informal policy for the temporary employment of Middleton high school students during summers and holidays. The temporary employees perform minimum-skill jobs in the company office and in the packaging plant. They are paid the federal minimum wage. Over the past few years, depending on demand, the company has hired, on average, eight full-time and six part-time student employees on this temporary basis (see page 125). The policy of temporary hiring has proved successful for both the company and the community. Graff has gained energetic, loyal workers, and the town's youth unemployment figure has been reduced.

A potentially serious problem arose three weeks ago when Towne Bakery, another of Middleton's large employers, was destroyed by fire. The owners have decided not to rebuild. Consequently, ninety Middleton citizens are now seeking new employment. Several of these individuals, who are competent and qualified workers, have applied to the Graff Candy Company. However, Graff has virtually no employee turnover, and the student temporaries provide all the extra staffing required during peak production periods. Thus Alice Graff has not hired any of the former Towne Bakery employees.

A group of former bakery workers, frustrated that they should be without jobs while high school students are gainfully employed, send a spokesperson to a Middleton Town Meeting. He argues that Graff's temporary employees, just "kids," are supported by their parents and do not really need the jobs. The former bakery employees, he went on, "adults" who must work to support their families, should be given those Graff jobs. This speech captures the attention of the local newspaper publisher, who subsequently writes an editorial against Graff's hiring policies. The editorial refers to Graff's "lack of responsiveness to the community's needs" and suggests that Alice Graff should "consider people, not profits" in company decision making.

Alice Graff does not wish to abandon her support for Middleton youth in the form of temporary jobs. Nor is she willing to go public with her history of community gifts. At the same time, she is stung by the accusation of her company's cold-heartedness. She would like to avoid any further rift between Graff and Middleton citizens without compromising her own vision of community service (that is, the package deal of anonymous gifts and temporary jobs to young people). She does not want to take any action without first considering all possible ramifications for her company and the community. Hence she decides to ask an outside party, the Middleton Business Association, to consider the situation and give her its counsel.

## •••••••••••••• PROBLEM

Your small group is the ad hoc committee selected by the Middleton Business Association to analyze the Graff Candy problem. Your task is to prepare a nonpartisan report in which you present the facts of the situation and make a recommendation. Your report will go to Alice Graff for her consideration; however, she refuses to meet and talk with you.

## Assignment

Write a three- to five-page report analyzing the Graff Candy situation and recommending a course of action for Alice Graff. Format your document by addressing the following questions:

1. What exactly is the *problem* or problems in this scenario? (Be specific.)

2. What is the *history* of the situation? (Trace its development from the starting point to the present.)

3. What are the possible *causes* of the problem? (Consider both persons and circumstances.)

4. What are the present *effects* of the situation? (Consider the situation both from inside and outside the Graff Candy Company.)

5. If no action is taken, what are the probable *future outcomes* of the problem?

6. Given the above analysis, what *alternative courses of action* are available to Alice Graff to address the situation?

7. Among these, which *resolution* do you recommend, and why?

### Annual Monetary Gifts to Middleton Youth Programs

| Year | Amount |
| --- | --- |
| 1967 | $ 600 |
| 1968 | $ 603 |
| 1969 | $ 660 |
| 1970 | $ 700 |
| 1971 | $ 720 |
| 1972 | $ 760 |
| 1973 | $ 860 |
| 1974 | $ 900 |
| 1975 | $1,160 |
| 1976 | $1,220 |
| 1977 | $1,340 |
| 1978 | $1,300 |
| 1979 | $1,400 |
| 1980 | $1,800 |
| 1981 | $1,860 |
| 1982 | $2,000 |
| 1983 | $2,300 |
| 1984 | $2,600 |
| 1985 | $2,750 |
| 1986 | $2,770 |
| 1987 | $2,850 |
| 1988 | $3,000 |
| 1989 | $3,300 |
| 1990 | $3,370 |
| 1991 | $3,600 |
| 1992 | $4,000 |

## Temporary Full-Time/Part-Time Employees

| Year | Temporary Hires |
|------|-----------------|
| 1979 | 4 f.t.  1 p.t. |
| 1980 | 4 f.t.  2 p.t. |
| 1981 | 5 f.t.  3 p.t. |
| 1982 | 5 f.t.  3 p.t. |
| 1983 | 5 f.t.  3 p.t. |
| 1984 | 5 f.t.  3 p.t. |
| 1985 | 5 f.t.  3 p.t. |
| 1986 | 6 f.t.  3 p.t. |
| 1987 | 7 f.t.  4 p.t. |
| 1988 | 6 f.t.  3 p.t. |
| 1989 | 8 f.t.  5 p.t. |
| 1990 | 7 f.t.  5 p.t. |
| 1991 | 8 f.t.  5 p.t. |
| 1992 | 9 f.t.  5 p.t. |

# IN WHOSE BEST INTEREST?

•••••••••••••• **INTRODUCTION**

A business or industry may enjoy the unanimous support of its host community. By providing good wages and personal security, a company can undergird generations of families and even whole towns. However, the mere presence of a business or industry within a community cannot guarantee its acceptance or support. Citizens weigh the promise of jobs against any potential harm that the company may cause (for example, air or water pollution, toxic waste, or nuclear exposure). Community interests and industrial development intersect across a range of economic, social, ethical, and health-related issues. The public relations of any business demand understanding of and sensitivity toward all legitimate interests of a host community.

This scenario pits tangible profits and jobs in the present against intangible losses and harm in the future. Commercial, government, and private constituencies represent different viewpoints toward industrial development. You will be asked to weigh conflicting interests in the balance between corporate and community welfare. To accomplish this, you will need to do some research, form alliances with like-minded constituents, prepare a persuasive presentation, and listen impartially to the views of others.

••••••••••••• **SCENE**

United Chemicals, Inc., is an American corporation with divisions in twenty-three states and subsidiaries in seventeen foreign countries. It manufactures a wide range of chemical products including pesticides, herbicides, petroleum additives, and secret (classified) chemical agents under government contract. United Chemicals wants to open a new plant to produce herbicides and products under government contract in Chester, New Mexico, a small town in a poor county. Unemployment in Chester and its surrounding region tops 15 percent, well above the national average. A United Chemicals plant would represent 150 jobs, making it the single largest employer in Chester. The town council is so eager for the plant to locate in Chester that it has offered 120 acres of land without charge to United Chemicals.

Two weeks prior to the signing of final papers confirming the decision to locate United Chemicals in Chester, a tragic accident occurs at one of the company's Malaysian subsidiaries. A deadly chemical leak kills more than one hundred residents near the plant and causes untold health problems for many others. The executives of United Chemicals, a company with an unparalleled safety record in the industry, have offered to settle all medical claims and have assured the public at home and abroad that such an accident could not be repeated. Because of the classified nature of its chemical products, the company's safety report cannot be made public. In response to citizen anxieties in the United States, United Chemicals asserts in very clear language that *no such leak* could possibly occur at any U.S. plant.

A group of concerned citizens in Chester, New Mexico, decides to confront the town council with the possible dangers of inviting United Chemicals to locate a plant in their town. They do not feel reassured by the explanation of the chemical leak in Malaysia and are now unwilling to run the risk of a similar occurrence in Chester. For these individuals, the possible dangers associated with the new plant outweigh the economic benefits of more employment.

A second group of citizens, Chester business owners, perseveres in its support of the United Chemicals plant. Although not ignorant of the possible dangers, this group feels that the economic advantages are greater than the risks. The long record of industrial safety displayed by United Chemicals is sufficient to assure these supporters of the corporation's vigilance in protecting public health.

## PROBLEM

Can industry, in this case United Chemicals, be trusted to protect public health? Will industry be responsible citizens of a community, in this case Chester, New Mexico? Is the corporation's interest in profits greater than its civic interest in safety?

Unless some consensus can be reached among townspeople, the Chester Town Council is hesitant to proceed with its offer of free land to United Chemicals. Despite the obvious economic benefits that industrial development would bring, council members do not want to support any plan that will divide their community into factions. Hence a special town council meeting, open to the public, is called to air opposing views on the issue of United Chemicals building a plant in Chester. The council will make its decision after the meeting.

The class is divided into four groups:

Group 1:  town council

Group 2:  representatives of United Chemicals

Group 3:  concerned citizens against United Chemicals

Group 4:  business owners for United Chemicals

Groups 2, 3, and 4 will each be given 10 minutes to present their viewpoint to the public meeting. The only restriction to this presentation is the time limit; any legitimate means of persuasion (speeches, media, printed materials, and so on) is permissible. After each group has made its formal presentation (that is, after 30 minutes), the town council will moderate a 30-minute open discussion in which members of any group may interact by asking questions or rebutting earlier presentations.

When preparing your case, you will need to rely on (1) real cases of industrial-community relations, which you can research; (2) general principles of economic and political policy; (3) common sense; and (4) quoted testimony of expert witnesses, derived from research. Because no specific data on the Malaysian accident can be made public, the corporate representatives of United Chemicals may rely only on their general record of safety and their responsiveness to this tragic incident. A planning sheet is included on page 129 to assist in group preparation.

The role of the town council (Group 1) is to moderate the proceedings and to listen; the council is not an advocate for any position but a facilitator of consensus, if such is possible. After the public meeting, Group 1 will confer privately and make a final decision about United Chemicals. (The Chester Town Council is under no contractual obligation to go through with this industrial development.) The council will then announce its decision, along with a supporting rationale, using the sample form on page 130.

## STRATEGIC PLANNING   Preparing a Case

When preparing your case for public presentation before the Chester Town Council, consider the following questions and issues.

1. Are there other, real-world, cases of industry-community development that might serve as examples and guides to understanding the benefits or dangers of our deliberation? How might these be researched? (Consult weekly business magazines and daily financial newspapers.)

2. What general principles of industrial development and community welfare could offer guidance and safeguards in Chester's deliberations? Develop this case as a philosophical argument.

3. What common-sense precautions and promises might help to ensure public trust in this situation? Can you suggest mechanisms for community oversight in the planning and building of United Chemicals?

4. What experts might be called on to support your case? Search the industrial, business, and popular presses for authorities who have gone on record in related cases.

5. After compiling your case, what options do you have for making an effective, persuasive presentation?

6. What arguments might you anticipate from the other groups? How can these be countered during the open discussion session?

# Public Announcement

Town Council of
## Chester, New Mexico

By a vote of _____, the Chester Town Council
has made the following decision regarding the location
of a United Chemicals plant in Chester:

The Council's rationale supporting this decision follows:

PART FOUR

# MEDIA AND TECHNOLOGY

# TELEPHONE SOLICITATION

.............. **INTRODUCTION**

The most common electronic medium used in business is the telephone. It extends the range of the human voice so that a conversation with someone in the next office sounds the same as one with a person across the country. Except in the case of conference calls, the telephone is a medium of one-to-one communication. Its total reliance on oral messages makes a real difference from face-to-face interaction. Language and vocal qualities carry the total weight of a person's intention with a medium that disallows nonverbal signs. In this scenario, you will concentrate on the telephone as a medium for one-to-one persuasion by designing a pledge campaign. Then you will play both roles, campaign caller and potential donor.

.............. **SCENE**

Working individually, devise a telephone campaign to solicit funds in support of a charitable cause. You may make up your own cause (for example, medical research, emergency relief, scholarships). After choosing a cause, create a strategy for telephone solicitation. The time limitation is a 3-minute conversation in which to get an oral pledge to contribute money. Regardless of your cause, your campaign should seek pledges in the amount of $50.

.............. **PROBLEM**

Three communication challenges are posed by this scenario: creating a charitable cause; designing a telephone sales strategy; and executing your campaign effectively, raising as much money as possible. At each stage, try to take into account the nature of telephoning as a mode of communication. You will need to prepare a brief message that a stranger could understand immediately. Then work for a conversational approach that is likely to move a potential donor from disinterest to commitment. Remember: the total length of your conversation may not exceed 3 minutes.

### PART ONE

1. Create your individual cause.

2. Write out the first part of your telephone sales presentation word for word. It should take no more than 30 seconds to deliver. Write aloud, rehearsing and revising your composition to encourage a conversational style.

3. Create a worksheet of questions and comments that you might expect from the persons you will call. (They are all strangers to you.) Mentally rehearse your answers.

### PART TWO

1. During the actual simulation, your instructor will set up the callers in one room or space and the potential donors elsewhere.

2. Each campaign caller will be permitted to make a certain number of telephone calls soliciting support for his or her cause. In turn, each potential donor will receive calls, playing the role of a person whose support is being solicited.

3. Each potential donor will be allowed to contribute a total of $150 to the causes presented (that is, $50 to each of three callers). After all calls have been placed, each donor should fill out the form on page 135 and pledge his or her donations.

# Charitable Pledges

**Your Name:**

_____

**I pledge to support the following three causes:**

    **$50 for** _____

    **$50 for** _____

    **$50 for** _____

_____

**Signature**

# SELLING BUSINESS 1
## Radio Spots

•••••••••••••• **INTRODUCTION**

As the title suggests, this scenario finds you marketing not a product or a service but "business" itself. The selling of a concept ("Buy American" or "Look for the union label") occurs in the marketplace of ideas. Here, you will work in small groups to produce a 20-second radio spot encouraging high school students to consider a business major when they go to college.

**SCENE**

Your small group is an ad hoc committee of the National Organization of Business Students (NOBS), an honor society for high academic achievers among undergraduate business majors across the country. Standards for membership are very competitive, ensuring that acceptance is a symbol of real academic distinction. Your committee, appointed by the executive council of NOBS, is charged with the task of encouraging topnotch high school students to consider majoring in business when they attend university. The campaign is designed to promote business as the field of study for high school graduates of the highest academic abilities. Your task is not to compare the relative values of business versus other potential majors. Nor is your task to promote any particular college or university. Rather, the point is to sell business itself as a discipline that promises special challenges and rewards to honor students.

**PROBLEM**

Your committee decides to create and produce a 20-second radio spot as one of your marketing strategies. The spot will be targeted to radio stations nationwide that count teenagers as their primary audience. Your idea is to air the spot during news broadcasts on these stations. You are determined to produce a commercial that can have arresting appeal and memorable impact on a high school honors student.

## Assignment

Working in small groups, first determine the exact aim of your commercial. What precisely are you selling and to whom? Then write (see page 138) and produce a 20-second spot recorded on audio cassette.

## STRATEGIC PLANNING Script for Radio Spot

Title of Spot: "Business: A Major Investment"
Sponsor: National Organization of Business Students
Air Time: 20 seconds
Program Slot: News

| **Script** | **Sound** | **Seconds** |
|---|---|---|
| Spoken Words | Music/Effects | |

5

10

15

20

# SEE THE WORLD — ON RADIO

............... **INTRODUCTION**

The conventional way to sell a travel package is by visual enticement through photographs, slides, and video that show a would-be traveler the color, scenery, vegetation, architecture, entertainment, and overall beauty of a new place. The travel industries spare no expense when producing slick photographs for brochures, posters, and television advertisements. To hit every possible audience, travel companies also may advertise on radio. In this scenario, you will be faced with the challenge of producing a travel advertisement using only sound for the radio. You will substitute the ear for the eye, translating pictures into words, music, and sound effects. The assignment will call for you to expand the normal inventory of business communication skills by including creative writing, performance, and production. This is an experiment, so have fun.

............... **SCENE**

You will work in a small group that represents a committee of the Student Activity Board at your college or university. Through a local travel agency, the committee has arranged a special one-week trip to London at a very good price. The package includes round-trip airfare, lodging plus two meals per day, two West End theater tickets, and several sightseeing tours. If you can get fifty students to put up a $150 down payment, the total price per student will be only $950. The job of the committee is to get the word out about this fantastic opportunity.

A sure way to reach a large number of university students in your town is to advertise on the campus radio station. With its variety of easy-listening, rock, and classical music, the station's programming appeals to almost every taste. Even though committee members are inexperienced in radio production, the committee decides to try creating a 30-second advertisement.

**PROBLEM**

If you are willing to produce the radio spot yourselves, the manager of the campus station promises to run it free of charge as a public service announcement. All the committee has to do is produce a 30-second radio advertisement on a standard audio cassette. One other thing: you will have to designate whether the spot should run during an easy-listening program (that is, pop music), during a rock program, or in a classical music slot.

## Assignment ••••••••••••••••••••••••••••••••••••••••••••••••••••••••••••••••••••••••••••••••••

1. The group meets to discuss the possibilities for approaching this radio assignment. Begin by listing the alternative scripts you can envision. At the beginning, do not worry about how to produce the ad. Just brainstorm the possibilities.

2. Decide which kind of audience you want to target — the listeners to pop, rock, or classical music. Consider the size of each audience, the likelihood of finding interested travelers, and your group's ability to create an appropriate radio spot.

3. Create a script (see page 141) for your radio spot. Be sure to include the destination of the trip, its special features, the cost, and a deadline for making a deposit. In addition to words, consider sound effects and music. Remember: radio is an acoustic medium. Its only channel for communication is sound.

4. Produce your 30-second radio spot on audio cassette. When submitting it to the instructor, be sure to indicate for which programming slot it is intended.

## STRATEGIC PLANNING 1   Script for Radio Spot

Title of Spot:   "London for Spring Break"
Sponsor:   Student Activities Board
Air Time:   30 seconds
Program Slot: _____

| **Script** | **Sound** | **Seconds** |
|---|---|---|
| Spoken Words | Music/Effects | |

_____
_____
_____
_____     **5**
_____
_____
_____
_____
_____     **10**
_____
_____
_____
_____
_____     **15**
_____
_____
_____
_____     **20**
_____
_____
_____     **25**
_____
_____
_____     **30**
_____
_____
_____

# SELLING BUSINESS 2
## TV Spots

............... **INTRODUCTION**

In this scenario, you will produce a television commercial presenting an exemplary figure from American business. Like radio production, this assignment asks you to expand the conventional inventory of business communication skills. Yet with video technology becoming more widespread in the classroom, the office, and the home, not too far in the future business managers may be expected to communicate routinely through this medium.

............... **SCENE**

A new genre of television commercial was created during the American bicentennial year, a short video biography of great Americans. Now this type of public service memorial is commonplace, commemorating great artists, remarkable sports figures, and notable inventors or scientists. These women and men are chosen as cultural role models because they represent some breakthrough of enduring importance in American history.

Working in a small group, representing the National Organization of Business Students (NOBS), your mandate is to create and produce a 30-second TV spot commemorating some figure of notable accomplishment in American business. These spots, contracted to the major television networks, will be aired in prime time during American Business Week, a designation created by presidential declaration.

............... **PROBLEM**

NOBS has stipulated that you introduce your TV audience to the exemplary careers of lesser known figures, rather than sticking to the safety of household names. Production possibilities include, but are not limited to, dramatic enactment, narration, and photo montage.

1. Working in a small group, research the possible historical figures from American business that the group might select to commemorate. Agree on one, and register your choice with your instructor.

2. Conduct research on your subject, and submit a bibliography of resources from which information was drawn.

3. Write your script. (See the guidelines on page 144.)

4. Produce your 30-second biographical spot on video cassette. (See the guidelines on page 145.)

## STRATEGIC PLANNING **1**  Scripting a 30-Second TV Spot

**1.** What central concept or event do you want the audience to grasp about your historical figure?

**2.** What other figures or events that were contemporaneous with your personage might help the audience "locate" him or her in history?

**3.** What lasting impact or legacy did your figure leave in contemporary American society?

**4.** What single word or phrase might you use to aid the audience's memory of your figure's importance?

**5.** What visual image or images might be used to represent your figure's history or importance?

**6.** What music or other sound effects might enhance the production?

**7.** In summary, what one thing do you want the audience to know about your figure? Be specific. How can you communicate this information in a memorable way?

# STRATEGIC PLANNING 2  Preparing for Production

Write a shooting script using a three-column format, as shown below. The first column should include any words spoken by a narrator or characters. The second column notes all other acoustic features, including music and sound effects. The third column describes what the camera sees.

| Words | Music | Pictures |
|---|---|---|
| Actor's Script | Music/Sound Effects | Camera Shots |

**Words**
Actor's Script

_____
_____
_____
_____
_____
_____
_____
_____
_____
_____
_____
_____
_____
_____
_____
_____
_____
_____
_____
_____
_____
_____
_____
_____
_____
_____
_____
_____
_____
_____

**Music**
Music/Sound Effects

1.

2.

3.

**Pictures**
Camera Shots

Shot #1

Shot #2

Shot #3

Shot #4

Shot #5

# TV TALK SHOW

•••••••••••••• **INTRODUCTION**

In this scenario, you will work in a group representing one of the constituencies addressing the issue of commercial development versus environmental conservation. The forum of debate will be a national Public Broadcasting television talk show utilizing a panel discussion format. The assignment will require research, oral fluency, and personal persuasiveness.

•••••••••••••• **SCENE**

*Business Today* is a weekly, half-hour television talk show produced and aired nationally by the Public Broadcasting System. Panelists representing conflicting viewpoints are invited to address a topic of current interest. Discussion is moderated by a host, whose main concern is keeping the debate lively, to the point, and nontechnical (that is, suited to a general television audience).

The topic for this week's program is "How can the nation decide between conflicting values of commercial development and environmental conservation?" The subject seems especially timely because of recent controversies over offshore drilling leases on the West Coast, dams on recreational waterways in the Rockies, logging in the national forests of the Midwest and Southeast, and habitat preservation for endangered species in the Northeast. However, panel discussion is not limited to any particular case or region. Rather, participants are expected to address the issue generally, on a national policy level, and bring to bear examples from across the country and from various industries. Panelists who have been invited to participate in this program are representatives from business and industry, conservation groups, and the United States Department of the Interior.

•••••••••••••• **PROBLEM**

You will work in a group representing one of those three constituencies. Your first problem is to find in the popular press or in technical journals reports of current situations on which to build a case advocating your group's viewpoint. Regardless of your personal perspective toward this issue, you will be expected to adopt and defend an assigned position. The second problem is for one individual to give authoritative voice to your group's position as a panelist on the TV talk show.

## Assignment ........................................................................

### PART ONE

1. The class is divided into three groups representing industry, conservationists, and government officials. Each group decides what the likely viewpoint held by its constituency is.

2. Group members devise a research strategy to seek out and collect expert opinion, applicable laws, and visible cases to support the group's position.

3. The research task is divided among group members, who conduct their investigation.

4. One member constructs the group's argument from the information compiled, trying to balance expert opinion with case studies and common sense. Because the format of a panel discussion is looser than a formal debate, the importance of the evidence must be rank-ordered from most to least persuasive. Rank-ordering will provide the panelist with some guidance as to which information to include at what point in the program.

5. The group selects a member to serve as panelist.

6. The group rehearses the questions that the panelist is likely to encounter when confronted by opposing viewpoints.

### PART TWO

7. The class simulates the TV talk show by creating a studio set for panel discussion. Four chairs are comfortably arranged, one for each group representative and one for the moderator. (Your instructor will provide the moderator.) All other class members will form the studio audience.

8. A camera is set up to videotape the half-hour discussion.

9. The TV talk show is enacted. The moderator opens by inviting each panelist to make a brief position statement (no longer than 1 minute). Then, for the remainder of the program, questions are asked by the moderator or by other panelists. Try to avoid the extremes of stiff turn taking or a free-for-all. The ideal is to create a *focused conversation*. If time permits, the moderator may open discussion to questions from the audience.

10. After the videotaping, the class views the program and analyzes the strengths and weaknesses of each case as presented. (See page 149.)

# JOB APPRAISAL

## Talking About the Talk Show

1. Characterize the overall feeling of the program. Did it seem more like a formal debate, an informal conversation, a classroom discussion, a verbal brawl, or some other type of interaction? Be specific when citing moments in the program to support your characterization.

2. Did the interaction among panelists and moderator undergo marked change at any point or points during the program? For instance, was there a moment when things got heated up, cooled down, excited, or out of control? This question asks you to trace the conversational energy throughout the discussion. Again, be specific in referring to the videotape.

3. What issues seemed to emerge as most important in the televised discussion? Did some topics keep recurring in the comments of panelists?

4. Conversely, what issues, once raised, seemed to disappear from ensuing discussion?

5. Which moments in the program were most memorable to you? If there is consensus among class members in identifying memorable moments, what communication principles might be learned from their features?

6. Describe (don't evaluate) the roles played by panelists and moderator throughout the program. Did individual panelists function more as question-askers, information-givers, peace-makers, agitators, jokers, or other kinds of conversational facilitators?

7. If you were to engage in another televised panel discussion, what might you do differently either in preparation or in production to enhance your communication effectiveness?

# VIDEO RÉSUMÉ

.............. **INTRODUCTION**

The traditional résumé, a print document, may in the future be supplemented by video. Certain college applications already encourage submission of a videotape along with the printed form. A videotape permits the selection committee at a university or in a company to see and hear the candidate as well as read about him or her. In this scenario, you will experiment with the video résumé, marketing your credentials through this electronic medium. Your presentation of yourself by means of videotape permits a personal glimpse, a quasi-interview, that may lead to a phone call and, ultimately, face-to-face interaction.

.............. **SCENE**

Imagine that your class is the personnel department for a large, multinational corporation, USIG, a conglomerate of industrial, service, and hi-tech divisions. Given its wide-ranging enterprises, USIG has need of every conceivable business talent. As an experimental (and optional) strategy for initially screening applicants, USIG has requested job candidates to submit a 2-minute videotape along with a traditional résumé as a way of introducing their professional qualifications and career interests. This video presentation, the company hopes, can supplement conventional screening devices and show something of a candidate's personality and communication skills, qualities that are important to business success but difficult to assess in a print document.

You will have opportunity to submit an individual video résumé and, along with the rest of the class, to review video résumés of others.

.............. **PROBLEM**

Your problem, as a job applicant, is to produce a 2-minute videotape that presents your talents, interests, and personality in a persuasive manner. Then, switching roles to the corporate side, your task as selection committee member is to evaluate on a standard measure the apparent competence and appeal of job applicants as presented in their videotapes.

## Assignment ........................................................................................

1. Working individually, produce a 2-minute videotape (no longer) announcing your career objective and introducing your professional qualifications. There is no generic format for scripting or producing this videotape; each individual may customize a communication approach to his or her interests and needs. Remember: with this medium *everything* communicates, both *what* you say and *how* you say it — vocal quality, physical mannerisms, clothing, grooming, background, and eye contact. Work for a presentation that demonstrates your professional expertise, personal competence, and individual character. At every stage of preparation, test your plan against the impression you want to make. Keep it technically simple. (See page 152 as a guide to preparation.)

2. After all the videotapes have been produced, class members should adopt the role of selection committee member and view the video résumés in quick succession. You will then fill out a confidential response form for each presentation (see page 153).

## STRATEGIC PLANNING   Preparing a
Video Résumé

1. What specific impression do you want to make on this prospective employer? List the features of personal background, career objectives, qualifications, and attitude that you want most to communicate.

2. Brainstorm the possible approaches you might take to featuring the profile described above. What do you want to say? How do you want to say it? Is there a specific experience or anecdote that demonstrates the qualities that you want to feature?

3. Write out your verbal presentation in a conversational style. Try speaking it aloud as you compose. Although TV is an electronic medium, the impression it makes is "up close and personal." Think of this more as a conversation than as a speech.

4. What visual options are available to enhance your presentation? In what physical setting should you make the videotape? What clothes should you wear?

5. Experiment with the camera to find the best distance and angle of vision for a pleasing (in-focus) picture.

Remember: at every stage of preparation, test your plan against the impression you want to create. Keep it technically simple.

## JOB APPRAISAL

Response to
Video Résumé

*Confidential*

**Applicant's Name:** _____

**Evaluator's Name:** _____

Evaluate each qualification below on a scale from 1 to 5, with 1 representing the lowest achievement and 5 the highest.

**1.** How would you rate the clarity of the applicant's verbal presentation?

_____

1                    2                    3                    4                    5

**2.** How would you rate the candidate's professionalism in the visual presentation of self?

_____

1                    2                    3                    4                    5

**3.** How would you rate the candidate's overall communication style in terms of appropriateness and persuasiveness?

_____

1                    2                    3                    4                    5

**4.** On the basis of this videotape, would you recommend an on-site interview for this applicant? Why or why not?

# VIDEO FRANCHISING

·············· **INTRODUCTION**

This scenario presents a special kind of sales conference in which you will market a service franchise by means of television. Like "Video Résumés," this scenario anticipates the increasing use of video technology in business communication. To accomplish the assignment, you will need to customize a service, analyze its potential franchising market, and produce a 5-minute videotape introducing the enterprise. Then, switching roles from seller to buyer, you will hold a video sales conference and invest in franchise opportunities. The scenario calls on the full range of your business communication skills.

·············· **SCENE**

You are an entrepreneur with an innovative concept for a new service enterprise, Theme Parties to Go. The idea is to provide all the services required to throw a really great party: food, drinks, decorations, entertainment, and invitations. For every occasion (from elegant gala to homecoming bash), and for every budget (from big bucks to small change), you can provide a fun and attractive party package. What separates your service from the ordinary catering and entertainment competition is the concept of a "theme party." Your standard themes include "Team Parties" (for example, Chicago Cubs, New York Knicks, Atlanta Falcons, St. Louis Blues, Los Angeles Kings); "Movie Parties" (that is, characters and decorations from the latest Hollywood productions); and "Vintage Music Parties" (that is, tunes, style, and cuisine associated with a particular kind of music). In addition to these three categories, you offer a customized service to match the individual themes of clients.

You feel that the concept is widely marketable because of its uniqueness and practicality, its reasonable cost, its relatively low overhead, and its operational feasibility. After having successfully piloted the service yourself, you decide to market franchises to local representatives, targeting university towns.

As a marketing strategy, you want to produce a 5-minute videotape introducing your franchise idea to potential buyers. You will distribute the tapes free of charge at conventions of the tourism, restaurant, and hotel industries. You do not expect the videotape by itself to sell a franchise. You simply want to spark enough interest for a prospective buyer to inquire further by phone or letter.

## PROBLEM

You are trying out the idea of a videotape promo on an experimental basis and do not have the capital to hire a professional production crew. Your problem is to produce the videotape yourself, with the aid of your staff at Theme Parties to Go.

# Assignment

### PART ONE

Working in a small group, plan and produce your 5-minute videotape introducing Theme Parties to Go. (See pages 156 and 157.) Bear in mind that you are not selling the party service itself to prospective clients. You are selling the idea of a franchise to potential buyers. You need to excite them with the potential of Theme Parties to Go to make a profit in their local market. Although the "Scene" identified standard party themes, you may improvise on your own. One possible approach might include a brief enactment of a party to enliven the presentation of commercial facts and figures. If you choose to demonstrate a team party, for instance, select a local sports team (college or professional). If you choose a movie party, select a film that is currently popular or a classic from the past. If you choose to demonstrate a vintage music party, seek consensus among group members about the period and style of music preferred.

### PART TWO

After the videotapes have been produced, show them to all class members, who are now playing potential franchise buyers. When deciding which presentations to follow up on (see page 158), consider the plausibility of the franchise idea as presented, the feasibility of its operation, the credibility of its spokesperson, and its marketability to consumers. Follow up only on the presentations with great potential for solid management and reasonable profits. You may follow up on only two presentations.

## STRATEGIC PLANNING 1   Scripting and Producing a Franchise Videotape

1. As a group, discuss the services offered by Theme Parties to Go, the target markets for your services, their consumer appeal, and the potential attractiveness of this idea to local franchisers. Test one another's understanding of the concept itself by raising specific questions.

2. Brainstorm possible approaches to scripting your 5-minute videotape. Do not settle for the first idea that comes to mind, but get as many ideas as possible on the table for discussion. Then determine which scripting strategy you will adopt.

3. Outline the shooting script for your video presentation. Include an introduction, each step of the sales sequence, a summary, and an address or phone number for further inquiries.

4. Write out verbatim the introduction of your sales presentation.

5. Write out verbatim the conclusion of your script.

6. Determine the visual elements you want to include in your videotape.

7. What print features, if any, do you want to use (for example, address or phone number)?

8. What audio features (that is, music or sound effects), if any, do you want to use?

9. Create your script, using the three-column format shown on page 157.

# STRATEGIC PLANNING 2  Preparing for Production

Write a shooting script using a three-column format, as shown below. The first column should include any words spoken by a narrator or characters. The second column notes all other acoustic features, including music and sound effects. The third column describes what the camera sees.

| **Words** | **Music** | **Pictures** |
|---|---|---|
| Actor's Script | Music/Sound Effects | Camera Shots |
| _____ | **1.** | **Shot #1** |
| _____ | | |
| _____ | | |
| _____ | | |
| _____ | | |
| _____ | | |
| _____ | | **Shot #2** |
| _____ | | |
| _____ | | |
| _____ | | |
| _____ | **2.** | |
| _____ | | **Shot #3** |
| _____ | | |
| _____ | | |
| _____ | | |
| _____ | | **Shot #4** |
| _____ | | |
| _____ | | |
| _____ | **3.** | |
| _____ | | **Shot #5** |
| _____ | | |
| _____ | | |
| _____ | | |
| _____ | | |
| _____ | | |
| _____ | | |
| _____ | | |

## JOB APPRAISAL   Buyer Response Form

**1.** Of all the video presentations, which one would you be most likely to write or call? Why? (Be specific in explaining your rationale.)

**2.** Which presentation would you be second most likely to follow up? Why?

# VIDEO TRAINER

.............. **INTRODUCTION**

In this scenario, you will work on the teaching skills that are important to in-house training programs in business and industry. Specifically, you will devise a series of four interactive videos to teach perspective-taking as a communication strategy.

*Perspective-taking* is the fundamental skill you have used to enact all the scenarios in this book. The term means, simply, an ability to experience some situation from another person's point of view, to take on the other person's thoughts, feelings, and attitudes in an effort to understand multiple perspectives. The role-playing encouraged by these simulations has constituted a major learning objective in itself, along with the specific communication skills in writing and reading, speaking and listening, interviewing and small groups, media and technology. Indeed, this perspective-taking ability is at the root of all human communication. Until you and I can look at things from each other's viewpoints, we have little chance of finding common ground for interaction.

Perspective-taking is a complex skill. It involves attitude, imagination, intelligence, capacities of language, and situational sensitivity. Despite the complexity, however, it is a skill that can be learned and taught, though it requires constant practice. It is also, arguably, the greatest predictor of success for a business manager or executive. Negotiations, sales, personnel development, policy formulation, and group decision making all depend on perspective-taking.

In this scenario, you will design your own interactive video simulations to teach the communication skill of perspective-taking.

.............. **SCENE**

Imagine that your entire class is the training staff of BCI (Business Communications Incorporated). Your company sends trainers into business and industry to lead communication workshops for every level of corporate employee. The training staff designs these workshops. You have decided to try out a new curricular idea for teaching perspective-taking. Your staff will produce a series of brief videotapes simulating two-party conflicts in face-to-face business interactions. Unlike a typical drama, your enactments will go only so far, leaving the audience to discuss possible resolutions to the crisis. Your teaching theory is that, in order to discuss the communication problems entailed in the video drama, your workshop participants will have to engage in perspective-taking, looking at things from both characters' viewpoints.

## PROBLEM

The scenario presents you with three problems: (1) writing a 5-minute drama focusing on some business conflict between two people in conversation, (2) producing the scene on videotape, and (3) writing a list of questions to be used by BCI consultants when they take your training videos on site to teach business communication.

## Assignment

1. The class is divided into groups. Each group brainstorms possible situations for a script (see page 161). Each training video should present a typical business interaction between two members of an organization. They should be in conflict. The video will take their interaction up to a point of crisis and then pose the question of resolution for the workshop participants (that is, the viewers) to resolve.

2. The group writes a script.

3. The group casts and produces a 5-minute videotape (see page 162).

4. The group writes a set of ten discussion questions to be used by the BCI consultant when leading an on-site workshop. The questions should help participants observe and evaluate perspective-taking abilities displayed in the video situation. Avoid asking simplistic questions that suggest their own answers.

5. The class views all videos and reads all discussion questions and evaluates their effectiveness as tools for teaching perspective-taking in business communication (see page 163).

## STRATEGIC PLANNING **1**   Designing the Script

**1.** Decide on the basic situation involving two characters in face-to-face interaction. Include enough concrete details for the viewer to understand the interpersonal dynamics without overcomplicating the scene. Avoid generalities and abstractions.

**2.** Create an individual profile for each character.

  o What is the character's name?

  o What is his or her function and title within the organization?

  o What motivates the character in this situation (that is, what does he or she want)?

  o How badly does he or she want it (that is, how far is he or she willing to go to get it)?

  o What is the character's attitude toward the other person?

  o What is the history of their relationship?

**3.** Specify points of conflict between the two characters in this situation.

  o Do they want different things?

  o Do they have different vested interests in the outcome of a situation?

  o Do they represent different divisions of a business organization?

  o Do they represent different levels of personal power or authority within the organization?

**4.** How do the characters' words reveal their individual perspectives and their interactive conflict?

**5.** How can you design the situation to lead to one central crisis, the point at which you will end the drama and invite viewer discussion?

# STRATEGIC PLANNING 2 Shooting the Production

1. In what physical setting does the drama take place? How can you simulate it? (Think carefully about how setting may influence interaction.)

   o Does it occur in the hallway (for example, at the water cooler)?

   o Does it occur in one of the character's offices? If so, which character?

   o Does it occur in a conference room? Lunch room?

   o Does it occur in a car? Commuter train? Airplane?

2. Cast the roles. (Think carefully about the possible perceptions associated with gender, age, and body type and how these may influence the dramatic interaction.)

3. Rehearse the scene in your stage setting. Work for plausibility by attending to detail. It is especially important to provide the actors with all the necessary props that might be used by their characters (for example, pens and pencils, file folders, legal pads). Such details enhance credibility and help set the actors at ease. Be sure the script is well memorized.

4. Videotape a final rehearsal of the scene. Check for the best possible camera angles, especially if the drama calls for action (for example, standing up or walking).

5. Videotape the scene.

## JOB APPRAISAL  Evaluating Post-Production

**1.** How plausible is the organizational setting of this conflict?

**2.** How believable are the two character profiles in the script?

**3.** How credible is the conversation between the characters?

**4.** How convincing is the enactment (that is, the videotaped performance)?

**5.** In what specific ways do visual elements of the videotape contribute to its impact? How do they detract?

**6.** For what specific audience would you target this videotape? Why?

**7.** How effective are the discussion questions in focusing the learning objectives of this videotape?

# Student Questionnaire

To help us plan for future editions of *Practicing Business*, please complete this page and mail it to:

**College Marketing**
**Houghton Mifflin Company**
**One Beacon Street**
**Boston, MA  02108**

1. Do the Scene and Problem sections of each scenario provide sufficient information for you to use in the Assignments?

2. Are the Assignments challenging and doable?

3. Are the FYI boxes, Strategic Planning worksheets, and Job Evaluation forms helpful? Do you have suggestions for improving these features or for adding others?

4. Which scenarios did you enjoy most? Why?

5. Which scenarios did you enjoy least? Why?

6. Please rate the scenarios below.

7. Please offer any other comments you would like.

|  | Excel-lent | Good | Fair | Poor | Didn't use |
|---|---|---|---|---|---|
| **Business Writing and Reading** | | | | | |
| Experienced Expediter Wanted | ____ | ____ | ____ | ____ | ____ |
| To Whom Are You Speaking? | ____ | ____ | ____ | ____ | ____ |
| Ghostwriting 1 | ____ | ____ | ____ | ____ | ____ |
| Get the Point? | ____ | ____ | ____ | ____ | ____ |
| A Chain Letter | ____ | ____ | ____ | ____ | ____ |
| Ghostwriting 2 | ____ | ____ | ____ | ____ | ____ |
| A Close Call | ____ | ____ | ____ | ____ | ____ |
| Politics and Profits | ____ | ____ | ____ | ____ | ____ |

| | Excel-lent | Good | Fair | Poor | Didn't use |
|---|---|---|---|---|---|

## Business Speaking and Listening

| | Excel-lent | Good | Fair | Poor | Didn't use |
|---|---|---|---|---|---|
| A Language Scavenger Hunt | _____ | _____ | _____ | _____ | _____ |
| Hospital-ity | _____ | _____ | _____ | _____ | _____ |
| Computer Game Sales Conference | _____ | _____ | _____ | _____ | _____ |
| Debate 1 | _____ | _____ | _____ | _____ | _____ |
| "It's My Party" | _____ | _____ | _____ | _____ | _____ |
| Debate 2 | _____ | _____ | _____ | _____ | _____ |
| Up in Smoke | _____ | _____ | _____ | _____ | _____ |

## Interviewing and Small Groups

| | Excel-lent | Good | Fair | Poor | Didn't use |
|---|---|---|---|---|---|
| Job Interview 1 | _____ | _____ | _____ | _____ | _____ |
| Job Interview 2 | _____ | _____ | _____ | _____ | _____ |
| Job Negotiation | _____ | _____ | _____ | _____ | _____ |
| Exit Interview | _____ | _____ | _____ | _____ | _____ |
| Affirmative Inaction | _____ | _____ | _____ | _____ | _____ |
| The Case of Infectious Research | _____ | _____ | _____ | _____ | _____ |
| Helping Hands | _____ | _____ | _____ | _____ | _____ |
| A Sweet Deal Turned Sour | _____ | _____ | _____ | _____ | _____ |
| In Whose Best Interest? | _____ | _____ | _____ | _____ | _____ |

## Media and Technology

| | Excel-lent | Good | Fair | Poor | Didn't use |
|---|---|---|---|---|---|
| Telephone Solicitation | _____ | _____ | _____ | _____ | _____ |
| Selling Business 1 | _____ | _____ | _____ | _____ | _____ |
| See the World — On Radio | _____ | _____ | _____ | _____ | _____ |
| Selling Business 2 | _____ | _____ | _____ | _____ | _____ |
| TV Talk Show | _____ | _____ | _____ | _____ | _____ |
| Video Résumé | _____ | _____ | _____ | _____ | _____ |
| Video Franchising | _____ | _____ | _____ | _____ | _____ |
| Video Trainer | _____ | _____ | _____ | _____ | _____ |

Thank you very much.

Your school _____

Your name (optional) _____